WHO DO YOU SAY THAT I AM?

A 52 WEEK STUDY OF THE NAMES OF GOD

CYNTHIA A. SHELBY

Flow DIVINE
PUBLISHING

ISBN: 978-0-578-96360-0

REVIEWS

"I am always looking for good Devotional Books to help me understand Jesus and God's love for me! When I started reading "Who Do You Say I Am?" I could instantly relate to Cynthia's stories from her own life and how God speaks to us through our everyday life experiences! My Bible knowledge also increased with each devotion as she bases everything on GOD's word! Cynthia is a gifted communicator and will help you grow in your understanding of God's love for you as you read these real life stories and scripture."

Greg Horn

Pastor of HOPE is Here Ministries, Lexington, Kentucky

"This devotional is one that will inspire women of all walks. It is so practical, yet so deep. The personal stories that Cynthia shares in these chapters that relate to the names of God are so encouraging and inspiring. This is a devotional that can be used over and over each year because there are so many names of God, that most likely we won't remember them all, but each time we read it God instills those names and meanings in our heart along with the scriptures she shares."

Rodetta Cook

Co-Founder Care for Pastors, Florida

"This book was one of the most refreshing devotional discoveries I've encountered. From the first day I began reading, I looked forward to a new story. The pages are filled with beautiful life lessons all connected to the many names and ways God shows himself to his children. It was authentic, relatable, and beautifully-written. I loved at the end of each crafted story, there was a connection to one of the many names of God as well as a prayer to pray. This book would make a beautiful gift to any woman of any age."

Tara Issacs
Review from Amazon. Educational Consultant

DEDICATION

First, I dedicate this book to my parents Rueben and (Lillian) Marie Allen who consistently poured their lives and nurture into me. I specifically think of my mother who was the first writer whom I admired in life. She wrote and published poems and I now write and publish my memories of her influence in my life.

Next, I further dedicate this book to my children Stan Jr. and Sydney. I gift you the stories of your parents and of my parents. I pray that you would read and value our stories and share them with your children. May this book be a legacy keepsake which keeps you close to the purpose of family and close to the God who ordained it. Continue our legacy by authoring truth and generously sharing as I, your grandmother, and aunts have in their lifetime.

CONTENTS

Seasons	9
Introduction	11
~WINTER~	15
1. Resolve for the New Year	17
2. Growing Up with Sisters	21
3. Time at the Table	25
4. Circle of Women	29
5. Granny	33
6. The Open Door	37
7. Seasoned Writers	41
8. In the Middle	45
9. Rhythms of Life	49
10. Black Not Dark	53
11. The Woman in the Mirror	57
12. Perfect Imperfection	61
13. Some Years	65
~SPRING~	69
14. Cha-a-a! Daddy! Cha-a-a!	71
15. Homemade	75
16. Noticed	79
17. A Vision for the Table	83
18. Baggage	87
19. Music Anyone	91
20. A Bannered Race	95
21. Core and So Much More	99
22. Spotlight	103
23. In Celebration	107
24. A Community of Doctors	111
25. Cherished Counsel	115
26. Manners	119

~FALL~ 123

27. Encircled 125

28. Moral Victories 129

29. Crowned with Glory 133

30. Eagles 137

31. All Gone 141

32. Mother "Sometimes" Knows Best 145

33. Encircled with Friendship 149

34. Noticed 153

35. Supreme Judge 157

36. Just Perfect 161

37. Forget Me Nots 165

38. When God Is All You Really Need 169

39. Determined 173

~SUMMER~ 177

40. Lessons at the Beach 179

41. From Masterpiece to Master Please Help 183

42. Childhood Imprints 187

43. Unseen Blessings 191

44. Anticipation 195

45. Liquid Gold 199

46. Right Standing 203

47. While I Wait 207

48. Invisible Goals 211

49. The Battle of Champions 215

50. The Economy of Mothers 219

51. Look Away 223

52. The Busy Burden 227

Notes 231

About the Author 233

SEASONS

Ecclesiastes 3:1-8 NIV

There is a time for everything, and a season for every
activity under the heavens: a time to be born and a time
to die, a time to plant and a time to uproot, a time to kill
and a time to heal, a time to tear down and a time to
build, a time to weep and a time to laugh, a time to
mourn and a time to dance, a time to scatter stones and
a time to gather them, a time to embrace and a time to
refrain from embracing, a time to search and a time to
give up, a time to keep and a time to throw away, a time
to tear and a time to mend, a time to be silent and a
time to speak, a time to love and a time to hate, a time
for war and a time for peace.

INTRODUCTION

If we hope to satisfy the "who or where" is God questions in our hearts, we must think deeper to explore the character of God as defined by His many names.

My first realization of the importance of a "name" was discovered at a professional baseball game in Milwaukee, Wisconsin. My husband and I had traveled for vacation to spend time with friends, originally from our hometown. We were warmly greeted by our hosts and by a city that brimmed with enthusiasm for baseball and beer.

The sound of pre-celebrations filled the huge parking lot, as tailgaters anticipated a victory! People of all races and ethnicities proudly draped themselves with the team's colors of gray, gold, and navy as they stood to enter "American Family Field" stadium. The energy was both eager and electrifying.

We were quickly led to enter through a secluded gate far right of the bustling ticket holders. I was in awe of the "moment" and did not say anything but wondered why our friends had led us beyond the familiar ticket lines, to enter through an isolated gate. Soon, we were greeted by an elderly gentleman in an official looking neon vest who directed us to an elevator.

Our friend, Jerry, stated that our names were left on a "family call list" as we approached an official looking table. Jerry did most of the talking and presented his name for the ticket call list. My husband and I held hands and stirred expectantly into the stadium. Our attention shifted from our friend to the stadium staff who mentioned there were no tickets left under his name.

The female staff manager leaned forward, as she listened to Jerry explain that he had a family member, of one of the coaches, with him. The lady blinked to a puzzled look and asked for the family member's name. My husband spoke up humbly and mentioned his brother, who was a Milwaukee Brewers coach. After a quick computer search, she conveyed, "Oh, I see THAT name listed here." We were directed to enter the waiting elevator without any further questions. I took a deep breath as I gazed at our reflections in the elevator panels and discovered something about this "elevator moment."

I internalized the power of a name. It was my husband's last name or our last name, which granted us access past the table, to the elevator, into the ballpark for our reserved seating. Our friend Jerry was well meaning but did not possess the credentials which allowed us "free access" into the ballpark. However, the name "Shelby" brought clarity to the female staff manger and granted us access to both the elevator and to our reserved seats.

Likewise, exploring the names of God in this devotional will bring you to "elevator moments" like mine." These memoir-styled devotions and targeted prayers are designed to answer your heart's questions as well as to usher you into a deeper understanding of God's character. Consider me your hostess to your reserved seating where you can enjoy a weekly studies with personal applications and spiritual insights about 52 of God's names. Imagined that we have just arrived at the floor of your personal growth and the doors are now open for your acceptance to your reserved seat. Will you join me?

~WINTER~

Isaiah 55:10-11 NIV
As the rain and the snow come down from heaven, and do not
return to it without watering the earth and making it bud
and flourish, so that it yields seed for the sower and bread for
the eater, so is my word that goes out from my mouth: It will
not return to me empty, but will accomplish what I desire and
achieve the purpose for which I sent it.

1

RESOLVE FOR THE NEW YEAR

In recent days, my sphere of friends has enlightened me on their perspectives for the New Year. I am reminded that a good friend can teach me whatever life fails to teach me.

Recent conversations revealed that my aspirations for the New Year may need some revamping.

One friend divulged her resolve, from that previous year, to eat a little chocolate every day and was quite pleased with her progress. I was entrained by the thought but, knew I lacked the genes to pull that resolution off without weighted regret.

Another friend shared her inspirations for new meal planning. She let me see a picture of a pot of chocolate fondue encircled by a plate of waffle pieces, crispy treats, sliced bananas, strawberries, and pretzels. Her motto for this New Year was "Eat Dessert First!"

I was provoked to think deeper about their New Year's resolutions, although I was highly amused at their honesty. I questioned myself, "Why can't I resolve to be motivated by stating what I will do versus what I won't do for the New Year?"

My mind raced to construct a whole list of "positives behaviors" which were well-suited for amazing resolutions such as: stretching before exercising each week, planning a date with a friend at least once a month, or being available to watch sunsets or sunrises regularly.

Fresh energy began to surge through my Spirit, as I thought about "enhancing" my life, rather than "correcting" it. Motivation began to swell within my mind, as I began to reconstruct my revised resolutions.

I contemplated the abundant living mentioned in the Bible and further questioned myself. "How much better would my days be, if I resolved to spend time with Jesus before meeting the demands and expectations of the day?"

So, I transformed my morning shower into my own prayer closet. I then pretended that my commute to work was my studio time, where I could sing familiar worship songs to the Lord. I resolved not to surrender time to the pressing demands of the morning, but to surrender my time to the One who is responsible for all life because He is the God of My Life (El Hayyah Psalms 42: 8).

Prayer

Heavenly Father, I resolve to acknowledge you more this year. Help me to put you first each day that you give to me life here on earth.

Amen.

El Hayyah – The God of My Life

a. Psalms 139: 13 – 16

b. John 3: 16

c. Job 33: 4

d. Romans 6: 23

e. Psalms 42: 8

2

GROWING UP WITH SISTERS

Growing up as the "baby" of five siblings and the last girl born in the family had its privileges. I had five mothers in a sense. My four sisters mothered me along with my natural Mom.

It is during holiday meals that I learn the most about how I grew up. Each of my sisters has stories about how they helped me acclimate to the world.

My oldest sister was the quintessential mother-figure who assisted Mom with meal distribution, hair combing, and all activities related to general care. She was a very responsible teenager who was groomed to be mindful of others and she did it well. There were a few mishaps related to properly preparing hotdogs, for the consumption of toddlers, but other than that she was amazing.

Next, was my sister who was the sensitive middle child. She always had great affection for me. Once, while emptying trash cans, she discovered a miniature pony-tail securely wrapped in white toilet paper. She quickly put her detective skills to work and began her search. I was the one with the missing ponytail and she quickly passed the information on to the household authorities along with the hard evidence. She also prepared me for the realities of womanhood when it was time for me to know.

Last was the sister who preceded me. We were closer in age and played together often. I remember my interactions with her the most. Memories of board games, jacks and swimming come to mind immediately. On one occasion, I remember her rescuing me from some scary waves which were drifting me to the deeper end of the pool. It was a frightening experience because I had not learned to swim yet.

In each instance, I depended on my sisters to help me in my growing years. They all "mothered" me and provided what they could when they could. Each one of them knew different facets about me.

I had and still have an amazing bond with each one of them. We can take great comfort in knowing that the bond we have with Jesus is stronger than any human bond we could ever experience because, He is our Creator and knows everything about us (El Deah Proverbs 15:3).

Prayer

Heavenly Father, thank you for placing people in my life who genuinely cares for me and about me. Today, I give you all the care within my heart and mind because you are my Creator who can embrace each care. Lord, help me to share my cares with you daily.

Amen.

El Deab – The God of All Knowledge

a. 1 Samuel 2: 3

b. Romans 11: 33 – 36

c. 1 Corinthians 1: 18 – 31

d. Proverbs 1: 7

e. Nahum 1: 7

3

TIME AT THE TABLE

I would guess that every woman has a unique routine which preserves her "me time." I justify that need for me by thinking, "It helps me balance it all and still stay sane." I am referring to my coveted morning hours. My mother was an early bird, and I inherited her genes, because I emerge from sleep, most days, without an alarm clock.

My internal programming is set for rising well before dawn, where my chase for the "table experience" begins.

A morning shower infuses my circuit board with power. Once in this mode, I select my scent for the day through the choice of deodorant, lotion, and perfume. I then head to the closets where pieces of my personality hang, in three separate locations. Options are vast, but my frequent choices are comfy-casual or classic church wear.

Soon the hunt begins for the right accessory. As an artist, I imagine my creative finish, well before my search for the right look begins. Some days, it is a one-of-a-kind jewelry set while other days it is a mod-ish scarf or a signature pin. Either way, my sonar leads me back and forth from my darkened bedroom, where my husband sleeps, to my well-lit master bathroom.

Hair and makeup are always reserved for last because it employs another set of creative juices. My descent to the table is paved with a set of carpeted stairs. I mentally decide then if the day will be better supported with rain boots, a stylish heel, or an open-toe flat.

A flick of the light switch confirms the start of the day. I confess, this is the "sweet spot" of my day. The sweet-ness of this spot has nothing to do with location or décor but has everything to do with it being the "space" where I am purposely alone.

In the stillness of my mornings, there are no phone calls, no permission slips to sign and no external distractions. The silence allows me to hear my own thoughts and to discern specific direction for my day.

Each morning is different, although the enchantment at the table is the same. There, I pay bills, design invita-tions, and address Christmas cards. At other times, I write, grade papers, and develop blueprints for my ladies' Bible studies. However, my most cherished time, at the table, involves spending time with the Lord.

At the table, I sip a cup of hot tea or sip a cup of coffee, as I am strengthened by Him. Daily, I strive, and I crave to know the Christ of the Bible. Daily I long for the Christ of the Bible to know me because He is the Lord My Strength (Jehovah-'Ez-Lami Psalms 28:7).

Prayer

Heavenly Father, help me to realize that you are always with me and help me to remember to be a woman who seeks your strength, from time spent with you.

Amen.

Jehovah-'Ez-Lami - Lord My Strength

a. Psalms 28: 7 – 8

b. Exodus 15: 2

c. 1 Samuel 17: 4 – 11

d. Deuteronomy 31: 6

e. Psalms 59: 16

4

CIRCLE OF WOMEN

Growing up, the baby of the family, was a unique experience. Most of my dearest memories involve my three older sisters. I had three very nurturing sisters who mothered me as well as my mom.

I was carefully reared in what I would call a circle of mothers. They caused me to grow up quicker and wiser than my peers.

Their care was tailored to fit me specifically and I grew to treasure it throughout my adolescence. When I left their circle another one was waiting for me.

I met another circle of women as I transitioned from grade school to college. The next circle of women who befriended me were my female professors. My new acquaintances were   professional women who taught me how to survive and succeed in college.

Their mentoring was so effective in my life that I credit them for the tenacity to navigate through degree programs several times and for having the vision to help further my education.

After college, I landed my first professional job, as a teacher. Again, there was a cluster of veteran women who showed me how to care for children and to teach them everything from appropriate behavior to where to place the comma in a sentence.

They coached, corrected, challenged, and celebrated me, sometimes all on the same day. Many of them are retired now but, the influence from that circle of women has shaped me into the educator I am today.

Again, in my church family, God has encircled me with a collection of women who handle me with great care and respect. Some women, I have known from my awkward arrival into ministry thirty-two years ago and others I have gotten to know from our brief interactions while attending conferences.

Either way, I have established relationships which have anchored my soul in Titus 2 precepts which have generously taught me how to authentically love both my husband and my children. I have emerged as a Godly woman within the circle of those women, God's precious handmaidens.

Looking back, I have learned that the Lord sends an array of people into our lives to encircle us with care, admonishment, rebuke as well as safety. He is a gentle Shepherd who knows exactly what we need and the right influences to lead us to our destiny (Jehovah Raah Psalms 23:1).

Prayer

Heavenly Father, you are my Shepherd. Continue to lead and guide me through the circle of people whom you send into my life. Lord, help me to recognize those whom you send and help me to learn from their divine instruction.

Amen.

Jehovah Raah The Lord My Shepherd

a. Psalms 23

b. John 10: 14

c. Ezekiel 34: 11

d. Matthew 18: 12 – 14

e. Isaiah 40: 11

5

GRANNY

Womanhood provides for us a plethora of gifts from puberty to long past menopause. One such gift is the blessing of your children's children.

Fond memories swell within me, when I think about my experiences with my "Grandma" and my "Granny." It is funny to think that those two names are now "at risk" of becoming extinct. My family and friends are now choosing to be called Grammy, Nana, Nia, Nanny, Mimi, and Gigi by their grandchildren.

Grandmothers today have renamed themselves because they still look and still feel young. The technologies of modern medicine, hair coloring and gym workouts cause grandmothers to blend in with the rest and thus they have renamed but have not repurposed themselves. Grandmothers know their role and will always know how to hold a special place in the life of a child.

I remember my dad's mom, whom we referred to as "Grandma," as a quiet silver-haired woman who wore flowery printed dresses and who loved to treat herself to chocolate covered cherries.

Memories of my mother's mom, whom we affection-ately called "Granny," are the most vivid in my adult life. She was not wealthy or degreed but, she was well versed in the fine art of "grand-mothering."

Granny was a cook from "scratch" type of woman. She had a chili recipe that I loved, because it had the right blend of tangy and sweet. Sugar was the secret ingredi-ent for many of her dishes because everything oozed with sweetness at her house.

Our breakfasts were the best! She would serve crispy bacon, scrambled eggs, and buttered toast with straw-berry preserves along with her famous coffee. I felt so grown up to have coffee! I remember it being sweet, creamy, and tasting more like hot chocolate.

Her afternoon soap operas were accompanied by hand crafted snacks of buttered popcorn or sliced apples and cheese. She sat in her comfortable chair, while I perched myself next to her on the twin bed covered with a knot-ted white comforter. Atop her bedspread, I entertained myself by checking the bumpy imprints on the back of my legs from the comforter, when the soap operas became boring.

I just remember my time with her as being special and awesome. I knew He loved me. Similarly, I think about how tenderly the Lord provides and daily shows His love to us. His special ways show Him as the Awesome God that He is (El Hannora Psalms 42:7).

Prayer

Heavenly Father, give me eyes to see all the awesome blessings like protection, kindness, and the abundant life you provide for me as well as a heart to express daily gratitude to you for it.

Amen.

El Hannora – The Awesome God

a. Deuteronomy 10: 17

b. Nehemiah 9: 6

c. Psalms 68: 35

d. Nehemiah 1: 5

e. Psalms 66: 3

6

THE OPEN DOOR

Three days have passed since my last workout and my arms still hurt. The push and pull, to raise myself from seated positions, had been my only exercise as I recuperated.

I chauffeured my daughter to her 6:00 pm appointment and decided to occupy my wait with an exercise class to loosen up a bit. I consulted an app on my phone and became interested in a kickboxing class nearby.

I like to work out more in the later part of the weekend to atone for second helpings or moments of weakness related to homemade desserts. I quickly calculated the calorie-burn of a Friday night workout and envisioned the guiltfree consumption of French fries or chocolate!

However, leaving the gym erased any thought of food. It was an excellent work out, but much more intense than I had anticipated. The sequence of gloved punches and kicks, to the bag, had brought my body to the point of total exhaustion.

It was now Monday and my body continued to reprimand me for Friday's decision. I decided to give the kickboxing class another try, at a different location and with a different instructor.

I dressed for class and added water, yogurt raisins and a protein shake to my gym bag for an after work out reward. Once at the gym, I took the steps to the second floor to wait with the others, for the doors to open. Arriving early, typically gets you a choice spot on the back row. Slothful late comers are always "rewarded" with the front row.

The open doors signified that it was time for class. I hung my hooded jacket on the rack and placed my water beside me. I turned around to discover the instructor from Friday night's class was teaching at this location, too. My heart sank and my body hurt at the thought of more torture.

Rhythmic sounds filled the room as we boxed this time without gloves or a punching bag. We worked out through a series of jabs, crossovers, and upper cuts timed to music. Further, we bobbed, weaved, and alternated kicks with our choreographed punches.

I totally enjoyed the experience this time and felt amazing walking out the same door I had feared entering an hour ago. I was reminded that I am presented with many doors in life, and it is up to me to seek the

best ones to enter. I am so thankful that the Lord was
an open door that I once pursued and through that
experience I now enjoy both a new and an eternal life
because He was an open door in my life
(Egō eimi hē thyra Matthew 7:7).

Prayer

Heavenly Father, give me strength to walk through open doors without fear and help me to hope expectantly for new experiences as I put my trust in you.

Amen.

Egō eimi hē thyra - The Open Door

a. John 10: 7

b. Psalm 24: 7

c. Matthew 7: 7 – 8

d. John 10:9

e. Revelation 3: 8

7

SEASONED WRITERS

Cloudy fall mornings mixed with seasonal rain can be a sedative to my Spirit. My morning appointment trumped my overwhelming desire to sleep in on Saturday.

My warm shower removed the chill from my bathroom and set the day in motion. I grabbed a vegetable drink and draped my body with a jacket, scarf, and rain boots.

I made strides up the leaf-covered steps of the literacy center. It reminded me of how I scrambled up those same steps years ago, when it was the local Public Library. My Mom was an avid reader, who frequently took us downtown to browse for books on Saturdays.

Once inside, I used the paint chipped handrail to steady my balance down the steps and to establish solid footing for my damp rain boots.

I heard voices seeping from a room near the end of the hallway. My nerves were bit on edge because I did not know what to fully expect. I gripped my writer's bag and entered the room with as much confidence as I could muster up.

A petite blond lady, dressed in a cowl neck sweater sat in the middle of the class. The student in me, chose the seat directly in front of her. I examined the room with the anticipation of locating a familiar face, although each one was more unfamiliar than the next.

We read the opening pages from our manuscripts, or they did. I had not penned my writings chronologically so, I declined to offer to read aloud. I listened quietly among the seasoned wordsmiths. Creative magic spilled from page to page, as authors shared from their heart's work.

Each reading was as diverse as each author. I was surrounded by a community of writers whose ages ranged from youthful to mature. Some were composed and read at a whisper, while others read with piercing passion. Narratives of romance, science fiction, historical fiction, and nonfiction all sat around the table beckoning for my attention.

I resisted the urge to compare and allowed myself to remember the Parable of the Talents. The number of servants who used their talents received increased. Unlike those who hid their talents and lost what they had. My mind reasoned to measure my talent with others, although my Spirit reminded me that

I was a "one-of-a-kind" creation of God. In that moment, I realized that there was not a mold for Him nor for me. I have merit not because of my talents, but because the Lord who had fashioned me in His image (Yahweh Exodus 3:14).

Prayer

Heavenly Father, help me to appreciate that I am your artistry. Help me to value all the talents you put within me and around me.

Amen.

———

Yahweh – I Am

a. Revelation 1: 8

b. John 8: 23

c. Acts 9: 5

d. John 14: 6

e. John 9: 5

8

IN THE MIDDLE

Arriving at the middle of any endeavor is a worthwhile feeling. I tend to celebrate my movement beyond the starting blocks and tend to pace my tasks to a creative finish.

My morning routine has developed a similar ebb and flow. After my dash to the table to write I head upstairs for hair and makeup. A quick breakfast and lunch prep are my next priorities soon after I have mastered my look for the day.

On a good day, I am seated behind the wheel of my car a little after seven, heading for work. However, a late start means that I will have to contend with traffic and will have to strategize for the "middle."

Getting out of my neighborhood often reminds me of the birthing process. I realize that it is necessary, although it is not always easy. My daily goal is to cross an opposite flow of traffic to get to another lane which follows in my desired direction. At the entrance of my neighborhood, I study the string of head lights surging from east to west looking for a break in the pattern.

Some mornings I am blessed by school bus drivers who stop the cross pattern of traffic and graciously allows me to make my left turn. At other times, I sit prayerfully calculating my next move.

When the traffic closest to me begins to trail off a bit, I gain courage and cautiously creep to the middle section of the street. It is in this place that I briefly celebrate how God parted the white sea of lights for me and think forward about the rest of my journey.

From the middle, I quickly shift my head to get a good over the shoulder view of the oncoming traffic. I scan the pairs of lights, looking for the right opportunity. Sometimes, an angel of mercy shows up and flashes headlights to signal my entry into the desired lane.

My maneuver through life feels much like my quest for the middle section of the street. I occasionally find myself in a place that God did not ordain for me to be. In my attempt to rescue myself, I sit motionless in the middle of my decisions thinking of what to do next.

While I am thinking, my Heavenly Father is ushering angels into my path to show mercy, or He is shining a distinct pattern of lights for me to follow. I encounter a handful of blocked roads and detours in life, but I

remind myself that it is my job to seek the paths illumi-
nated with His light because He is the Lord My
Light (Jehovah-Ori Isaiah 42:16).

Prayer

Heavenly Father, thank you for being the Light of the World. Help me to seek you when I need light and direction in life.

Amen.

Jehovah-Ori - Lord My Light

a. Psalms 27: 1

b. John 8: 12

c. Psalms 37: 5 – 6

d. 1 John 1: 5

e. Psalms 119: 130

9

RHYTHMS OF LIFE

Treating myself to my favorite television dance show has been the perfect after dinner dessert for years. My excitement would build throughout the day as I thought about famous celebrities, shining costumes, amazing sets, and themed music. Each season was always different and the level of competition never disappointed.

Backstage glimpses of both the training and the knowledge of choreography helped me to appreciate the amount of work associated with each dance.

I have been watching the show for so long that I feel like one of the esteemed dance judges. My television-trained dance eyes would study each performance and would mentally score the couples much like the in-studio judges.

Each dance had its own personality with its unique series of well-crafted steps paired with melodious music. The atmosphere was always electric! The choreogra-phy was always well crafted and caused me to connect the dances to real life.

The events of life can either lunge me forward or halt me to a sudden stop. For instance, the "Jive" is a fast paced and soulful dance. Its lively movements are executed with sudden swings and hops which remind me of seasons where everything is accelerating way too fast, and it feels difficult to catch my breath.

Some parts of life resemble the "Viennese Waltz" where I struggle with being stagnant. In some seasons situations have embraced and rotated me around and around in circular motions. In these seasons, I weakly confront habits and people who sweep me from my past to my present with little to no grace. I find myself repeating and recalibrating into a familiar ca-dence which prevents me from progressing forward.

Without warning, some life seasons tempt me into a sultry "Rumba" where my passions cause me to move aimlessly into calculated abandonment. I feel myself reaching and grabbing for things I want. Desire consumes me as I toy with risky thoughts and allow myself to be pressed into compromising decisions. I partner myself with the wrong cares which leave me with heavy regret.

Varied rhythms of life can distract my attention away from focusing on the Lord, who always leads me as a skilled and protective dance partner. As a loving husband's affection can be protective and can be provoked to jealousy, so is the nature of the Father God (Jehovah Qanna 1 Corinthians 10:22).

Prayer

Heavenly Father, help me to keep my eyes on you as I transition through life's rhythms. Help me to depend upon your sufficient grace to partner me through any situation.

Amen.

Qanna – Jealous God

a. Exodus 20: 4 – 5

b. Psalms 135: 4

c. Exodus 20: 9 – 11

d. Matthew 22: 37

e. Luke 16: 10 – 13

10

BLACK NOT DARK

My husband and children made me aware of their growing concerns during dinner. They inquired about my wardrobe. I looked down and assured them that my wardrobe choice had nothing to do with me being depressed or mourning in any way as I was wearing black.

Most would agree that black compliments any figure nicely and black projects the illusion of a slim silhouette. A woman who thinks this way will make sure that she has plenty of black outfits for occasions like class reunions and speaking engagements.

I secretly began to build a defense for the case of "black," as I sifted through my master closet. My unconscious collection disclosed that I had more than a "little" black dress. I saw black pants, black leggings, black vests, black dresses, black shirts, black jackets, black workout gear and other black items which had hidden themselves among the other colors of clothes.

My memories cannot pinpoint when I began my love affair with the color black, although I do recall being fascinated with it right out of college. I was trained, as a young sales associate, to lure consumers, by presenting all diamonds on a black velvet pad. The bigger jeweled necklaces were placed on black velvet necks within our cases. Brilliant lightening brought each piece to life as it sparkled and glistened.

A Caribbean cruise summers ago taught me to enjoy the color black at another level. My curiosity, after a midnight trip to the rest room, led me to the balcony of our stateside room. I was held hostage from sleep, as I watched the moon brighten the inky sky and show its reflection upon the darkened ocean. Breathlessly, I stood watching the moon polish each wave.

One of our most memorable dates took place at a black-tie charity event! The choice of my husband's ebony double breasted suit was an easy choice along with his black bow tie. I matched him with a sable-colored cock-tail dress covered with black sequence. I loved our outfits and randomly allowed my eyes to feast on a parade of other black outfits throughout our dinner.

On the contrary, there is darkness, in the spiritu-al realm, that does not appeal to me at all. I love to wear black but have no interest in the darkness which can settle in the heart due to sinful acts. It makes me thankful for Jesus' death on the cross and for the Holy Spirit He left here on earth to assist us as God Our Helper (Elohim Ozer Li Psalms 54: 4).

Prayer

Heavenly Father, thank you for your sacrifice on the cross. And for the Holy Spirit. Teach me to rely on Him daily in every area of my life.

Amen.

Elohim Ozer Li – God My Helper

a. Acts 2: 38

b. John 14: 20

c. Luke 1: 35

d. John 14: 16 – 17

e. Psalms 40: 17

11

THE WOMAN IN THE MIRROR

Certain selections of music, on my cell phone, transform my ordinary bathroom into a sanctuary filled with melodious sounds and a spirited atmosphere. I felt His presence as I applied my make-up and thought about the morning's worship service. I mumbled, "Yes, my heart is yours Oh God!"

A series of cell phone dings and pings interrupted my private service and distracted my attention from Him. Unable to resist, I escape from my bathroom sanctuary to check my recent text messages.

The reverent aurora drained from my head and settled into my heart. A dear friend had been in prayer and had decided to send me a text, with multiple probing questions.

My thumbs defensively responded. Our exchange lasted so long that I completely forgot about my choice of lipstick and the time. I waved for my husband and children to leave without me, because I was unable to separate myself from the ongoing text conversation.

My emotions surged from anger to arrogance, from hurt to humility and then from recognition to repentance. I was exhausted and now late for Sunday service.

I seated myself atop the nearest pew "the toilet" to process my friend's line of questioning. As a southern lady, I had made all the right decisions that morning regarding pearls, perfume, and pumps. However, I was not prepared to go beyond the "mirrored image" as I sensed the Lord was leading me.

Both sighs and tears poured from me as I prepared my heart to surrender at the altar of truth. Smudges of make-up showed on the toilet paper I used to pat around my eyes. Christ wanted me to know the real condition of my heart this morning.

Unforgiveness had entered at some point and had hidden itself behind both rationalization and hurt. My wound had scabbed itself with quiet and was completely undetectable to me. It hid itself from morning prayers, daily scripture readings and regular visits to church.

I stood to face the woman in the mirror. I needed forgiveness from my Heavenly Father at this point. I painfully confessed what was in my heart as tears dropped into the sink. His healing power embraced me immediately.

After my "altar prayer" I allowed the music to play once again and segue wayed into "benediction." I sensed the Lord was protecting my soul from the weeds of unforgiveness which had grown in the garden of my heart. In that moment, I was reminded that Jesus is the Lord that heals our hearts with love and compassion (Jehovah Rapha Jeremiah 17:14).

Prayer

Heavenly Father, give me eyes to see the unseen things in my heart like unforgiveness. Help me to confess my shortcomings daily, so that you can bring healing into my life.

Amen.

Jehovah Rapha – The Lord Who Heals

a. Psalms 30: 2

b. Isaiah 53: 4 – 5

c. Psalms 103: 2 – 4

d. Matthew 8: 5 – 17

e. Luke 8: 43 – 48

12

PERFECT IMPERFECTION

Early in our friendship my now husband would randomly stop by my parent's home to bring me "I miss you" cards or my favorite flavor of ice cream. Our late evenings spent on the telephone often ended with me falling asleep and he never got upset about it.

As friends, I was determined not to develop a romantic interest in him. I found him different from others who pursued women like conquests. He just showed up at church one day and over time we became the best of friends. Time proved that he was the kind of person who could support to my dreams, my fears, and my inferior thoughts.

Through prayer we both sensed that God had a bigger purpose for our friendship. It felt unusual, but I allowed God to show me how to transform His love from affectionate to romantic.

Our engagement was as calm as the friendship we shared. It consisted of a simple midweek proposal in a downtown park at dusk. There were no outward whistles or bells, but we both knew that our prayers had been answered.

I learned that responding to the Lord's leading was not a simple fix. I had dreamed, like most little girls, that falling in love with the right person would cause everything to flow perfectly.

Although I had said yes, I secretly had my share of doubts. I wondered why he picked me from the collection of single ladies at our church. What was so special about me? I was educated, but some ladies had more education than me. I was active in the church's ministry, but so were other ladies. In all honesty I worked out some, but others had better figures than mine. I pondered also about our "packages" which included our families and goals, because they were much the same.

The carefree confidence displayed during our friendship began to corrode during the early months of our engagement. I do not know if it was the constant study of "perfection" depicted in all the bride's magazines I was reading or if it was my mind trying to align my childhood dreams with my now reality. Whatever the case, I just could not figure out why a guy like him would be interested in an "imperfect" girl like me.

My insecurities surfaced and dissolved as I got to know him better. It reminded me of my relationship with

Christ. He, too, is interested in "imperfect people" like me. He knows my education, my interests, my dress size as well as my family history and is still interested in a relationship with me. The Lord is not interested in the outer appearance, but He, like my then fiancé, is interested in my heart. I know that the Lord saw our hearts at that time and wanted to justly bless us with a Godly marital union because we chose to do this His way (Jehovah Gmolah Hebrews 11:6).

Prayer

Heavenly Father, help me remember that I am called to walk by faith and not by sight. Further, help me to recognize that you are a just rewarder of those who diligently seek you.

Amen.

Jehovah Gmolah – The Lord Who Rewards

a. Matthew 6: 6

b. Luke 6: 35

c. Matthew 6: 17 – 18

d. Luke 6: 38

e. Colossians 3: 23 – 24

13

SOME YEARS

Calendar cycles have a regularity all of their own. January to December is a travel map with many pathways and destinations. Some years I voyage through months with ease and finesse. In other years, I traverse through difficult months which slow my pace. Whatever the case, I end up at the same place, the holidays.

Regardless of the path that brings me through the year, December and the celebration of Christ's birth is sure. I think of the story behind the nativity and can identify with the range of emotions, I imagine were associated with the "first" Christmas.

Sometimes I have approached the holiday like Joseph. I know what is expected, but still wrestle with the thoughts and opinions of others. I need divine inspiration to shift from depression to peace to joyfully share the season with others.

I have also dealt with the fear that the Angel of the Lord produced among the shepherds. Unexpected expenses have surfaced, casting a cloud of worry and anxiety over my budgeting. I struggle to be a blessing and resort to the sacrifice of personal gifts to afford presents for everyone.

Regal magi carried gold, frankincense, and myrrh as they searched for the Christ Child. Some years allow me to shop for the best gifts for my family and for my friends. I can plan my shopping list with thoughtful consideration and can track down the right gift well ahead of time.

Other years, I have experienced the preoccupation of King Herod, who was distracted from the promises of the coming Christ. I have allowed my attention to divert my heart from the celebration of Christ due to the hectic schedule of Christmas plays, parties, and preparations for family gatherings. I have found myself losing focus for the season by centering on lesser events.

I find myself having to retreat into meditative thought to tap into the jubilation that the angels must have felt at the announcement of the coming Holy One. I've had to center, my heart, on the gift of Jesus Christ in the earth to avoid the commercial stress which veils the season.

In other moments, I have imagined the heart of the virgin Mary, who had to carry the promised Child.

From the moment of conception, she had to learn to be a loving guardian, like the Lord's love for us.

He loves us as The Strong Creator God that He is (Elohim Genesis 1:1-12).

Prayer

Heavenly Father, grant my heart focus, throughout the year. Help me to both embrace and to honor your presence within me regardless of the season.

Amen.

Elohim – The Living God

a. Psalms 109: 26

b. Deuteronomy 6: 4

c. Genesis 1: 1 -12

d. Psalms 82: 6

e. John 10: 34

~SPRING~

_____

Song of Songs 2:11-13 NIV
"See! The winter is past; the rains are over and gone. Flowers
appear on the earth; the season of singing has come, the
cooing of doves is heard in our land. The fig tree forms its
early fruit; the blossoming vines spread their fragrance.
Arise, come, my darling; my beautiful one, come with me."

14

CHA-A-A! DADDY! CHA-A-A!

We became parents later in life. We had grown accustomed to our own schedules and were surprised at the amount of sacrifice it took to rear a child.

My mother had one "later-in-life-baby," but solicited help from my four older siblings. The expansion from a family of two to a family of three was significant for me. We meticulously selected the best daycares, practiced the alphabet with flash cards and made sure we took our little guy to children's church regularly.

Our church held Easter egg hunts and we wanted our son to have that experience, too. The "threes" and "fours" were permitted to search the lawn first to capture colored eggs lying in plain view, because they would never find them hidden.

Once our son's tiny basket was full, we headed back inside for a light lunch and more giveaways. My son obtained a golden egg which made him the proud owner of an oversized stuffed lamb. He hugged and squeezed it all the way home that day.

We soon learned that the lamb would become the fourth member of our growing family. My husband used it to entertain our son in the evenings, while I cooked dinner.

Squeals and giggles drew me to the doorway of our great room one evening. I watched my small family of "three" playing on the floor while dinner simmered on the stove. The woolly lamb was the same size as our three-year-old and he played with it like a brother.

My husband would grab the lamb and pretend to wrestle our son with it. He made the lamb come to life with martial arts moves and the sounds of "Hi Ya!" Our toddler would burst into laughter as my husband playfully made the lamb brush over his face and tummy.

Immediately, he would get back up and press the lamb back into my husband's hands and say, "Cha-a-a! Daddy! Cha-a-a!" We understood that to mean that he wanted to play one more round of "Hi Ya" with his dad.

Watching my son's endearing interaction with the lamb and his daddy caused me to think about our Heavenly Father. God has an intimate father-like love toward us to feel as His dear children (Ab/ Abba Psalm 68:5).

Prayer

Heavenly Father, help me not to wrestle with sinful acts which lead my heart away from you. Help me to surrender myself to your fatherhood without hesitation or guilt.

Amen.

Ab/ Abba – Father, Daddy

a. Proverbs 3: 11 – 12

b. 1 Corinthians 8: 6

c. Ephesians 4: 6

d. Psalms 68: 5

e. Isaiah 64: 8

15

HOMEMADE

Mother did it all without the help of Betty, Sara, or Marie. She was skilled in the kitchen with simple ingredients like flour, sugar, eggs, salt, butter and sometimes a little yeast. Her labor was long, but we all were partakers of the reward.

In our home meals, cookies, pancakes, cakes, pies, cornbread, and breads were all homemade. Mom cooked from her heart, so recipes were rare in our kitchen.

She had her unique specialties, but her warm buttery yeast rolls were the best! As a child, waiting through this process was challenging. I did not understand that there was a method to obtain the spongy yeast rolls we all loved.

It felt like an entire day would pass with me watching her experienced hands mixing, kneading, sculpting, and positioning the dough in a bowl. Soon it was time to form the swollen dough into cute little balls and to place them in muffin pans with brushed butter.

My wait was pacified by playing close to the kitchen. The combination of those simple ingredients bolstered a smell that would fill the entire house.

On tip toes, I stretched myself to peek at the rolls' progress although my stature only afforded me a quick glimpse of the light shining from the oven window. I am sure mom's view was much better, and she always knew the moment when they reached their golden-brown readiness.

Mom would typically have a full audience as the curtain rose for her closing performance of bread making. The aroma of the baked bread magnetically drew all of us to the kitchen. We fixed our eyes on the tiny heaps showing above the rim of each pan. We anticipated her next act with moistened mouths.

Her final performance involved placing pats of butter in the center crease of each yeast roll and lightly coating each top with butter as well. Our hearts would stand at attention as we waited for her invitation. We knew that the homemade delights were for dinner but understood that free samples would be distributed to those who showed up early for the pre-show.

In our home, my mom's warm yeast rolls had the reputation of being both tasty and nourishing. Just as I waited for the loving kindness of my mother for natural food, I can be expectant for the God of My Kindness, Goodness and Faithfulness to provide to be spiritual food for me as I walk through this life (Elohay Chasdi Psalms 59:17).

Prayer

Heavenly Father, thank you for being the Bread of Life. Help me to ingest your kindness, goodness and faithfulness as nourishment each day. Let your presence serve as my daily bread.

Amen.

Elohay Chasdi - The God of Kindness, Goodness and Faithfulness

a. Exodus 34: 6 – 7

b. Ephesians 14: 17

c. Roman 11: 22

d. Psalm 34: 8

e. 1 Corinthians 10: 12 – 13

16

NOTICED

A high-quality diamond reflects the collective brilliance of many well-cut facets. My colleagues, my church family, and my best friends all enlighten me, but it is the time spent with my circle of family which causes me to shine bright and be strong in the world.

I spend time with my dad, and it is always pleasurable. My visits may find him enjoying his morning coffee, preparing for Wednesday night bowling matches or watching his favorite sports teams on television. His strength teaches me the value of simplicity as we sit to catch up on work, the grandchildren or money matters.

Moments with my siblings are equally as special although not as frequent. My brother is always on the go and we connect for brief seconds while driving from place to place. Our visits are often short and to the point. His strength challenges me to think and causes me to see life through a whole other lens.

On the other hand, I get to spend more time with my sisters and our relationships could be compared to an aromatic bouquet of flowers. Each one emits her own fragrance into my life as we enjoy our sisterhood. I glean from them all as they model for me home-making, hospitality, ministry, and new techniques for teaching. Their strength inspires me to do more, say more and be more as a woman.

Quality time spent with my immediate circle of family impacts me as well. My children require a lot of teaching and guidance daily. In all honesty, they strengthen me by teaching and guiding me during our shared meals and weekends of fun together.

I am strengthened further as a woman in quiet times alone with my husband. It is rare that we can sneak away from the children for meaningful bonding. We intentionally connect while getting ready in the mornings or before bed at night. He adds a different vantage point, to my life, as he offers his male perspective to my thoughts and ideas. He cultivates within me the value of femininity and provides a peaceful balance.

I naturally reflect the beauty of these positive relationships from my family circle along with the strength which flows from each of their personalities. Similarly, there should be reflections of strength which are evident from my time spent reading scripture or praying. As a result, our lives should reflect His powerful influence as much as moments spent with our circle or family. Those who know you should be able to sense something different about you as I reflect your relationship with a Strong and Mighty God (Jehovah-'Izoa Hakaboth Psalms 24:8).

Prayer

Heavenly Father, help me to prioritize spending time with you and cause my life to shine forth your attributes so that others may see you in me.

Amen.

Jehovah-'Izoa Hakaboth - Strong and Mighty God

a. Isaiah 9: 6

b. Zephaniah 3:17

c. Ephesian 6:10

d. Deuteronomy 10: 17

e. Joshua 22: 22

17

A VISION FOR THE TABLE

We dreamed of buying our first house as newlyweds. Our search was short for the simple fact that we were wide-eyed and clueless about buying a home.

Our choice was an older construction in a quiet subdivision, mostly comprised of seniors and retirees.

Somehow, the "charm" began to fade as we learned more about the maintenance needed for our "new" investment, which was older than both of us. The cost of replacing the heating and air system, replacing the outdated wallpaper, and restoring the hardwood floors was a challenge to our meager repair budget.

The impact of sacrificing for five years, for remodeling, caused us to look for another home. This time, we were prepared and were savvy enough to ask the realtor crucial questions.

Again, we decided upon a quiet neighborhood, although these homes were much newer, and the home-owners were close to our age.

I'm a woman of artistic vision, so I began sketching my plans for each empty room. I solicited help from an interior decorator, who happened to be the mother of one of my middle school students.

At our invitation, she wandered eagerly through our home consulting my sketch pad dreams and making comments about our home's potential. We had spent so much money fixing up our first home that we had little money left to buy furniture. Most of our rooms were bare.

I guided her to the formal dining room, and she stood motionless in the middle of the carpeted room. She admired the only piece in that room, which was a beautiful glass-topped cherry wood dining table. Her conversation shifted and she shared a vision of women sitting around this table someday. I smiled and politely nodded as my heart skipped a beat, because I so wanted ministry in our home. Her words echoed again in my Spirit years later, when I held my first Bible study around that table.

Since then, I have taught numerous Bible studies to women from all social classes, around tables of every kind, and from coast to coast. It is hard to imagine that a woman, whom I had met casually, became the catalyst for me finding my place around the table. This memory reaffirms that the Lord will make known His purpose for our lives because He is the Creator of our lives (Jehovah-Bara Isaiah 40:28).

Prayer

Heavenly Father, give me eyes to see and ears to hear from those whom you send into my life to speak your purposes and highlight destiny to me.

Amen.

Jehovah-Bara – Lord Creator

a. Romans 1: 25

b. Nehemiah 9: 6

c. Colossians 1: 15 – 17

d. Ecclesiastes 12: 1

e. John 1: 3

18

BAGGAGE

While rushing to the trunk of my car, to toss in my gym bag, I made an important discovery. The disarray on my front and back seats reflected my current state of mind, as well as some newly developed habits.

Most people would not have thought much about my car-clutter. However, God allowed me to discern more than the "untidiness." He allowed me to really see that my multiple handbags were signs of an overly scheduled life! I paused for deep thought as I stood to grasp my door handle.

I thought, I am on the "go" the second my feet descend to the floor, until my body surrenders well before the nightly news. My mind is thoughtlessly set on auto pilot as I live from bag to bag.

Monday through Friday is my daily grind of writing, working, and workouts. Similarly, the weekends are reserved for ladies' Bible study, church, and meetings with my mentor. Whatever the schedule, I tote each bag from place to place. My weekly activities are aligned according to my bagged agendas.

Any teacher worth his or her salt has a bag full of mostly ungraded papers, school calendars, red grading pens, and other related tools for teaching children. After a full day of work, we escort these bags home to complete more work. We routinely transport these bags back and forth from school to home whether we have the energy to take them from the car or not.

Admittedly, I have two workout bags. One is prepped for "water fitness" class and the other is prepped for walking the track or group exercise classes. I typically leave these packed bags near my front door for motivation.

Once a week, I grab a purple draw string bag to take with me to the clinic. The Diabetes Prevention class meets regularly for weigh-ins and nutritional support. The contents of this bag include a food-calorie book, fat reducing recipes and a binder for our weekly health lessons.

A favorite bag of mine is a multi-colored shoulder bag. I begin my mornings with this bag and then chauffer it to the public library or to the mall's food court, to meet with my writing mentor once a week. An array of colored pens, pencils, devotional drafts, and a full-sized legal pad live in this bag.

My most cherished one is a slender black bag outlined with sequence cross. This bag is a daily "go to" for me. I surrender to its wisdom regularly as I reach for my Bible to read or study.

Observing my car caused me to see the excessive of baggage in my life. Similarly, Christ was sent to humankind to deliver us from the weight of life's natural and spiritual baggage because He is the Lord my Deliverer (Jehovah-Mephalti Psalm 18:2).

Prayer

Heavenly Father, help me prioritize carrying your scriptures within my heart first, so that I can better manage all other bags of responsibility in my life.

Amen.

Jehovah-Mephalti - The Lord My Deliverer

a. Psalms 18: 2

b. I Corinthians 10: 13

c. Psalms 34: 17

d. 2 Peter 2: 9

e. Psalms 50: 15

19

MUSIC ANYONE

My dad stopped over one weekend right at the end of the school year to visit us. He came in and found his usual spot in the kitchen.

While we were growing up, the kitchen was our "grand central" station. It was the place where Mom would prepare each meal with love, the place where I completed my homework and most importantly it was a gathering spot for family for every reason.

He seated himself at the head of the table, which was his custom in our homes and immediately asked where the grandchildren were. Soon they graced the doorway and after a session of kisses and backrubs our visit began.

I love talking to Daddy, it is always calm and familiar. I informed him that his grandson had started playing the clarinet and his granddaughter had started playing the violin this year. Without hesitation, he called for my daughter Sydney. I was unsure what he was up to, so I sat back to watched the exchange. He asked if she could play him a song. My heart smiled as I continued to listen.

She quickly ran upstairs and returned with the needed apparatuses. She carefully unfolded her music stand and positioned her book in the center of it. Next, she lifted her violin from its case and cradled it in her arm to tune it. Last, she skimmed the book for the right song. Soon, sweet sounds flowed from the instrument. Once finished, she bowed, and he clapped! I watched the two of them and squeezed back a tear. It was so precious.

Admittedly, it was a good kitchen performance although it was "screechy" at times. My Dad did not care, he was completely engaged. Peacefulness emanated from him that day as his ears were entertained with both pleasant and unpleasant sounds from her tiny violin. Similarly, Jesus is the same way. He is with us daily, sits in our presence and offers peace to all who call upon Him (Jehovah Shalom Philippians 4:7).

Prayer

Heavenly Father, I call upon you today to settle my heart and to distract me from everything that is happening around me. I pray that your peace will guard my heart and mind today

Amen.

Jehovah Shalom – The Lord Is Peace

a. 2 Chronicles 20: 29

b. Isaiah 9: 6

c. 1 Corinthians 14: 32

d. Philippians 4: 7

e. Romans 16: 20

20

A BANNERED RACE

Watching the Olympics is always a guilty pleasure which keeps me up too late and challenges my morning perkiness.

One night, I found myself rushing through my evening routine in hopes of climbing into bed with my stack of ungraded papers, a red pen and my cherished remote.

My excitement heightened, as the lineup of sporting events was announced. I soon lost interest in grading papers and centered my attention on track and field events.

I have never participated in an organized sport and cannot really say that I fully understand the rules associated with most of them. However, I was electrified by the cheering fans, bright lights, multi-colored flags, and focused athletes.

My interest quickly fell upon a row of female athletes preparing for a hurdle race. Each pre-race routine looked different but, all the women were gazing toward the finish line set before them.

I sensed their anticipation and secretly prayed for no injuries. The mishaps during the hurdling events can be some of the worst to watch. I leaned forward at the sound of the starting gun's "BOOM" to witness the string of ladies unravel toward the finish line.

As a novice spectator, I stopped tracking which country was in the lead and became more intrigued with the "race" itself. I noticed that each lady was positioned in her own lane, ran at top speed, and stretched herself inches above the tiered hurdles.

It reminded me that each of us has been given a unique race which requires us to compete individually while being surrounded by a team of competitors. We run at our own personal best and stay flexible enough to avoid situations which could disrupt or destroy our race.

Each athlete had purposed to run a good race and to finish strongly with the hope of parading her country's flag of victory at the race's end.

In an equivalent manner, our spiritual races should be focused on God's set pace as we stride from glory to glory toward our destiny. Our eternal desire should be to display the Lord as our Banner of Victory in every race in our lives (Jehovah Nissi Psalms 20:4-6).

Prayer

Heavenly Father, strengthen me as I run the race which you have called me to run. Surround me with those who will push and propel me forward. Help me to stay focused in my own lane; lift my mind above obstacles and wrap me in your grace so that others may see that you alone are the one who causes me to finish in victory.

Amen.

Jehovah Nissi – The Lord My Banner

a. Exodus 17: 15

b. Numbers 2: 1 – 2

c. Psalms 60: 3 – 5

d. Jeremiah 51: 27 – 28

e. Psalms 20: 4 – 6

21

CORE AND SO MUCH MORE

"Only thirty minutes!" I thought as I happily reached for the pink yoga mat and a miniature yellow exercise ball. I walked across the room to search for a spot on the back row or somewhere near the corner.

Figures, all the good spots were already taken, so I plopped my gear and body in full view of the instructor. There will be no hiding today, I thought.

The instructor was petite, solidly built and full of energy. We began with stretches. I had not "really" worked out in some years but had decided that it was "time." I reached and pushed, and it felt good. Tension in my upper body began to melt into puddles in the presence of the calming music and breathing regimen.

Suddenly, the music tempo increased as the instructor led the class in a series of stationary poses. We were instructed to hold these positions and breathe. My arms and legs wobbled and teetered as I aimed to keep them steady. It was obvious, I lacked the balance needed to stay in one place like the rest of my class.

I set my gaze upon the instructor to avoid seeing my contortions and facial expressions in the mirror in front of me. Thirty minutes, who could do THIS for thirty minutes? I glanced at the clock on the wall and five whole minutes had passed. I looked up and whispered a tiny prayer.

I was not sure what I was praying about, because I really did not know what I needed. Did I need help to persevere, or did I need help to get out of this class? My pride would not allow me to concede defeat and place my equipment back into the bend and beeline for the door. I had to admit to myself, this core workout was challenging, and I was struggling beyond measure.

Fifteen minutes had passed, and I had survived all the standing poses. I had no idea what was next, but I was confident that the floor segment would require only the use of my back and or knees.

I was right. To my surprise though, the legwork was worse. I could feel firm carpet hairs puncturing my forearms and elbows. We soon rolled to our backs for crunches and sit-ups. I could feel the sweat trickle from my forehead to the corners of my eyes. I could not even muster the strength to wipe it away.

Twenty-five minutes had passed, and I realized two things. One, I totally lacked the strength for this "thirty minutes" core class. Two, I had to lean on the Lord to be my strength when I needed it the most because He is the Strong One (El Isaiah 40:29)

Prayer

Heavenly Father, help me to rely on your strength whenever I am weak.

Amen.

El – The Strong One

a. Psalms 46: 1

b. Jeremiah 16: 9

c. 1 Thessalonians 3: 13

d. Psalms 28: 7

22

SPOTLIGHT

I have allowed myself "binge behavior" for the sole purpose of comfort at times. On various occasions, I have spent the day over-shopping, catching up on seasonal melodramas, or eating too much of the normally restricted foods.

Feeding such appetites can be dangerously rewarding if you are open to self-discovery and are open to learning from life's classroom. One such discovery emerged when I treated my teenagers to an animated movie one Friday night.

After our outing, I spent the following morning researching familiar singing artists and songs which were featured in the animated movie we had watched. I binged on video after video, on my laptop and hummed those familiar songs, while eating breakfast.

My personal research led me to a series of live recordings from one of my favorite artists. I noticed something unique about his touring band, while enjoying familiar songs. Each gifted musician and singer seemed gen- uinely happy to serve as a background singer, so that the famed artist's genius could be highlighted.

I watched as trained and experienced artists fused their talents to create a platform where a featured artist could perform at an optimal level. I also witnessed the dynamics of the synchronized band and their impact on the audience which was phenomenal!

My favorite artist was gracious enough to direct the spotlight from himself to significant members of his band to highlight their instrumental solos. He even paused to acknowledge the musical aptitude of one of his background singers, who happened to be his beloved daughter. This concert segment finished with a tribute he had written in honor of her birth.

I was touched by his fatherhood. He shared her with his devoted fans, which he had collected for decades. They both stood on the same platform, and he shared his fan- base, so that she could ingest a bit of his fame.

I observed the two of them honoring one another before the world and was thankful for that binge experience, which taught me an important spiritual lesson.

The Lord created both the heavens and the earth for His good pleasure. He composed and orchestrated a symphony of life. He then allows us, His creation, to share in the riches of His universe. Then He stands back to allow us to develop our own talents. The stage was His, but He chose to share it with us because He is a Gracious God (El Channun Isaiah 30:18).

Prayer

Heavenly Father, thank you for creating a place for me in the world you created. Help me to always acknowledge you for the talents and opportunities you have placed in my life.

Amen.

El Channun – The Gracious God

a. Psalms 116: 5

b. Exodus 34: 6

c. Joel 2: 13

d. Psalms 86: 15

e. Psalms 145: 8

23

IN CELEBRATION

Looking at engagement rings, searching for the right dress and penning envelopes of wedding invitations is a faint, but cherished memory. My recollections usher me back to our special day at the altar.

Today was no different. I was both excited and nervous for our two friends. I was excited about their decision to deepen their relationship through the act of marriage, but nervous about attending a traditional African wedding where I did not know the expectations or protocols.

We sat in anticipation while watching the procession of parents, ring bearers, flower girls and the wedding party cascade down the aisle. It was so beautiful and romantic.

I noticed something different about the family members in the procession. They were making ethnic celebratory sounds as they came down the aisle. In response, the seated family members echoed the sound.

The pastor lifted his hands to signal a standing salute for the bride. She was a dream in every way. Her entrance was quiet, but her family and friends were not. Again, I heard the melodious sounds of what I believed to be ethnic congratulations. Unsurprised, she blushed at the sounds and walked slowly through their outstretched hands which extended into the center aisle.

During the ceremony, the two were asked the traditional marriage questions and each time sounds of celebration erupted. I was beginning to understand that African weddings welcomed participation as well as spontaneous praise.

Soon the new couple was introduced to attendees and proceeded beyond the sanctuary. They warmly greeted guests and family. There were lots of what I perceived to be traditional hugging, kissing and well-wishing as people trickled through the receiving line. I admired the variety of reds, blues and golds woven into beautiful style. Further, I was intrigued by the matching head wraps too, each unique and fashionable.

Guests did not leave the church right away, to head to the reception, instead they circled the couple for another customary event. This time, the sounds culminated into a song in their native tongue. Praise enveloped the atmosphere, as they sang in unison around the couple.

I was riveted by praise, as I listened to their rhythmic chorales of song. We are encouraged to make joyful noises and to continually offer up a sacrifice of praise to God which is the fruit of lips giving thanks. We are to live a lifestyle of praise and to be quick to express it to the God of Our Praise (Elohay Tehilati Psalm 109:1).

Prayer

Heavenly Father, thank you for the life you have given me and help me to always express praise to you for what you have done for me.

Amen.

Elohay Tehilati – God of My Praise

a. James 5: 13

b. Psalms 150: 1 – 6

c. Daniel 2: 20

d. Jeremiah 20: 13

e. Ephesians 1: 5

24

A COMMUNITY OF DOCTORS

Medical visits can be an extra expense when a family lives on a humble budget. Dad was the breadwinner of our family and Mom stayed at home with us. She took care of our primary needs with home remedies, and she took us to well-baby checkups, at the Baby Health Clinic.

In college, my commitment to wellness checkups was sometimes irregular, but I managed to get an appointment with the Student Infirmary when necessary. My inconsistent visits matched everything else, which was irregular about college-life like sleep, finances, and dietary planning.

My newlywed through my young mother years reset the dial for proper medical attention. I sought a variety of specialized doctors for family planning and infant checkups. My visits became regular once again and I endured lots of probing in honor of the "practice of medicine." I balanced appointments, immunizations, and other related inoculations that my career required. It was a memorable time of sticks and pricks.

Maturity introduced me to a new set of medical awareness. My primary care physician began scheduling yearly exams like mammograms, pap smears, and colonoscopies at age 50.

Years of standing on cement floors, thinly covered with carpet, initiated referrals with a podiatrists and vascular specialists. It was the vascular doctor who first suggested that shedding a few extra pounds may help to resolve my issue of varicose veins. I listened but did not change my lifestyle very much.

Several months ago, a routine blood glucose check-up yielded some untimely news. The matter was quickly assessed, and I was introduced to another branch of medicine which included nutritionists.

Nutritionists are not doctors, but I understood that they know the body's systems well enough to advise me toward better health and wellness. To me, I think of them as doctors when they help me to design a plan for a greater quality of life.

I was thankful for the unexpected diagnosis and thankful for the new community of doctors. Growing up in an affluent country, from infancy to maturity, had caused me to take quality health care for granted.

My community of doctors and their circle of continual care reminded me of my relationship with the Lord. The

Bible shares scriptures about God's care plan for me, to prosper and to be in good health as my soul prospers.

The scriptures are the Lord's written prescription which sets us apart for spiritual health just like the doctor's care plan set me apart for unique care. Christ is the Lord, who sets us apart for His intended purposes (Jehovah Mekoddishkem 11 Thessilonians 2:13).

Prayer

Heavenly Father, thank you for always being there to cleanse sinful acts and to set me apart for a healthy relationship with you daily.

Amen.

Jehovah Mekoddishkem – The Lord Who Sanctifies You

a. John 17: 17

b. 2 Thessalonians 2: 13

c. 1 Thessalonians 5: 23

d. 1 Corinthians 6: 11

e. 1 Thessalonians 4: 3

25

CHERISHED COUNSEL

Some of my greatest achievements are my best kept secrets. As a professional woman keeping record of my accomplishments is customary for advancement. However, as a mom, I daily perform specialized skills without much notable fanfare.

When my children were younger, I had both the energy and the passion to dress them with the precision of a doll clothes-maker. I was meticulous about my daughter's wardrobe because shopping for her required lots of attention to select dresses, to choose ruffled socks and to coordinate hair bows.

The shopping industry has changed, and I recognize that the twenty first century shopper has become accustomed to online sales, promotional codes, as well as shipping and handling fees. Fortunately, I still enjoy the physical experience of shopping and continue to do it in person.

For me, there is still a thrill associated with my seek-and-search missions to style my daughter. Once on site, I searched for her style which ranges from casual comfort to what she calls a vintage flare. I peruse the racks of clothes with a careful eye to wisely select items I think she would enjoy.

In the event of indecision, I snap a few pictures and text them to her. She soon responds with her favorite choice and off to the checkout counter I go. Our combined shopping technique allows me to shop at my own pace at the times that I desire and to have her input as well.

The real shopping joys begin once all the items are gathered at home in her room. During the week, there is little to no conversation about outfit selections. She selects what suits her for the day and delivers it to my bedroom for ironing.

Selections for Sundays or special occasions are quite different. At my request, she searches through clothing looking to match the right patterns and colors. Typically, I position myself atop my bed and wait for the style show to begin. I sit as a fashion judge to evaluate the pageantry of outfits which flow through the door.

I can offer constructive advice regarding seasonal needs, appropriate accessories, and the benefits of modesty for a young lady. She is always open and receptive to both my choice of clothes and counsel. In a comparable manner, I pray that I am always open and receptive during prayer to receive the Lord's choices and counsel. He knows the way of my footsteps and sends answers to me through the circles of people He places in my life because He is a wonderful, Counselor (Ya'ats Isaiah 9:6).

Prayer

Dear Heavenly Father, open my heart daily to your instruction and counsel so that I may fully know the plans you have for me.

Amen.

Ya'ats – Wonderful, Counselor

a. Psalms 73: 24

b. Isaiah 28 :29

c. Psalms 16: 7

d. Psalms 32: 8

e. Job 12: 13

26

MANNERS

Mom always taught me and my four older siblings to say, "thank you" and "please." Her five little ducklings were well trained with impeccable behavior and with biblical values. Her heart was anchored in the idea that a "good" mother should train her children to be both respectful and intelligent.

Others often rewarded us for our good behavior during church services. The scent of strong perfume always introduced the presence of her church lady friends. Their aged hands would reach deep into their large purses and produce wrapped rounds of peppermint goodness. When we were accepting our treat, Mom would lean close to our faces and utter, "What-do-you-say?" That was our cue to practice what we had been taught, which was to say, "thank you!"

Over the years, our mother modeled and displayed gratitude for blessings bestowed upon her and us with gracious words. Our household exuded the expectation of politeness, and we readily obliged.

During a routine visit, I noticed something different about Mom. She had always been quite the storyteller, but this evening she began to repeat herself. We also observed her constantly looking for her purse and other household items. Over time, her forgetfulness became unsettling.

It took some time before Dad would admit that Mom needed medical attention. As a family, we leaned on and upheld each other through appointments and diagnosis. The independence of our mom was ebbing away. Soon, she could not be left alone, because she would forget to take the muffins out of the oven on time or she would uncurl her hair right after my sister had rolled it up. Her spirit was the same, but her actions began to resemble that of a child.

We encircled mom with love, and we sought the best care for her. She always enjoyed people and did not mind regular doctor's visits. She pleasantly greeted receptionists and health care professionals. She even carried on a bit with her doctors. That was the mom we knew and loved. She was now caught between two worlds, and it was heartbreaking to watch her transition from a vibrant independent mother to an elderly dependent senior.

Dad lovingly organized her bedside care. We expressed our love through a rotation of feeding, baths, and personal caregiving. I noticed something remarkably familiar about my mom after our acts of love for her. She always remembered to say, "thank you." There were times when she did not even remember our names, but she never forgot to thank us. My heart clutched those words tightly because it was my best memory of Mom. She had changed, but our Heavenly Father will never change in His love and commitment toward us. He is the same today, tomorrow, and forever as we walk with Him through life's course (Lo Shanah Hebrews 13:8).

Prayer

Heavenly Father, thank you for creating me and never changing in your unconditional love and acceptance of me.

Amen.

Lo Shanah – The Unchanging God

a. Malachi 3: 16

b. Isaiah 55: 11

c. Hebrews 13: 8

d. Isaiah 40: 8

e. James 1: 17

~FALL~

Proverbs 6:6-8 NIV
Go to the ant, you sluggard; consider its ways and be wise! It
has no commander, no overseer or ruler, yet it stores its
provisions in summer and gathers its food at harvest.

27

ENCIRCLED

My body quickly adjusted from the brisk fall air to the warmth of the pool. Chlorine filled my nostrils and I was entertained with a circle of ladies dressed in swimwear. Some of them had silver hair, some had hair pulled into sleek ponytails and some, like me, had their crowns of glory stuffed under swim caps.

We gathered ourselves in the pool and quickly got started. Our water fitness instructor was quite upbeat and her style differed from most. I typically attend water fitness classes where we workout as individuals, but today, we were invited to pursue the water workout in a group.

Her routines required that we take hold of each other's hands to experience the support of a circle. I have never experienced this before. We pushed, pulled, and propelled ourselves on the waves. Seeing their faces, while working out, was quite different from looking at the backs of heads and bodies.

I kept thinking about the intimate circle as I showered and quickly got dressed.

I headed for the indoor track, to walk some laps, to give my daughter a few more minutes of water play. Enormous window panels surrounded the circled track. I observed the multi-colored leaves outside and the people who were gathered in twos and threes around the inside track.

My attention soon shifted to the basketball court below. The design of the indoor track allowed me to see the happenings from the first floor while walking on the second floor. I also noticed that girls of all ages gathered themselves in teams. They shared a basketball court as they circled for three on three and one on one games.

I was prompted to think back to a generation ago when women gathered in circles around the tasks of canning and quilting. There was a "want" and a "need" to come together. It was a celebration of human connectedness and the sharing of lives.

I thought deeper that day about the "need" to embrace life with others. God has purposed that we have life and have it more abundantly. We were created to need and to interact with each other as patterned by God's daily interactions with Adam, in the Garden of Eden. There is safety, comfort, and a sense of "belongingness" within the circle of others. God is the Giver of Life or the Creator that has designed for us to live life with others (Elohim Chayim Jeremiah 10:10).

Prayer

Heavenly Father, help me to walk away from distractions, which isolate me from the Body of Christ. Bring me "life giving" circles, of people, that I may better know of the abundance of life you have created for me.

Amen.

———

Elohim Chayim – The Living God

a. Jeremiah 10: 19

b. Psalms 42: 2

c. Joshua 3: 10

d. Acts 14: 15

e. 1 Timothy 4: 10

28

MORAL VICTORIES

I consistently choose not to look to the left or to the right, as I forged my shopping cart through the crowded aisles. Rarely have I associated holiday foods with the word "lust" or "temptation," but today I was hungry enough to confess such phrases.

My senses toyed with the idea of consuming the deli's fried chicken, the freshly baked breads and the Dutch apple pies displayed in cold cases. I resisted it all and channeled my bridled desires toward the checkout. I positioned myself to look at the tabloid headlines to avoid the allure of candy bars and chips while I waited for my turn before the cashier.

However, I rewarded myself with organic, lightly salted popcorn on the way home to celebrate a slight moral victory, although I was still mentally struggling with the sights and smells from the grocery store. I could have eaten every holiday trimming in sight!

The trip home was quick and so I was determined to get to the gym. I knew I should, but really lacked the motivation to get there. Thanksgiving was three days away and I needed a backup plan just in case my "grocery-store-will-power" failed me during the holiday.

My children must have detected my slothful body language and offered to accompany me to my workout. With reservation and hesitation, I agreed. I was not sure if two energetic teenagers would help or hurt my current situation.

Once at the gym, they completed a couple of track laps with me before heading off to pursue other adventures. I watched them move into the equipment room through the huge glass windows. Their workout looked more like "play time" but, I was happy to have them near me.

During the first mile, I entertained myself by keeping an eye on them. My gaze broadened to observe groups assembled for both Pilates and Zumba. I soon shifted my attention below to a basketball game comprised of elementary aged children. Their ball handling skills were amusing to watch and the perfect distraction to conquer my second mile.

I was eight laps into my third mile when my step counting device vibrated to signal my ten thousandth step triumph! I experienced a sudden boost of energy.

Again, my two gym mates returned to the track with carefree laughter and excitement. Just having them near me somehow strengthened me. I feel that same strength just knowing that God's promises are sure. I am reminded of the promise that states God will never leave me or forsake me, because He is the God who is always with me (Immanuel Matthew 1: 22 – 23).

Prayer

Heavenly Father help me to always recognize your presence and to honor your presence. Strengthen me daily as I walk with you through temptations of life.

Amen.

Immanuel – God with Us

a. Joshua 1: 9

b. Zephaniah 3: 17

c. Ephesians 3: 17

d. Revelation 3 :20

e. Matthews 28: 20

29

CROWNED WITH GLORY

My hands squeezed the tips of both armrests in the dentist's chair as I prayed silently. I have been a patient in this office, since I was in pigtails, and I have endured every procedure known to the human mouth.

The exploratory poking from both the hygienist and dentist, confirmed that God had answered my prayer requesting a temporary crown and not a root canal.

My return visit, to fix a chipped tooth, stretched the anticipated forty-five minutes into three hours. The sensitivity of my teeth caused my dentist to numb me repeatedly to fit me for the crown. Eventually the drilling and the numbing stopped.

I reached for my things and headed to the restroom, before scheduling my next appointment. My eyes locked to the image in the mirror. Oh no, my poor cheek and my poor lips! The numbing medicine pooled to the bottom of my cheek causing the corner of my numbed lips to slant downward. I was afraid.

Exiting the restroom, I expressed my concerns and fears directly with the dentist. She was unsettled, too, by my face and handed me a prescription for pain meds, an antibiotic as well as her personal cell phone number. She assured me that the numbing agents would take a while to dissipate from my cheek and in the event of a problem, I should call her right away.

Normally, the prescribed after-care would be no problem, but I was scheduled to be at a ladies' conference in two hours in another city. I quickly filled the prescriptions and put a cold pack in a plastic loc storage bag to ice my cheek through the drive.

Warm greetings and conference goodies were handed to me as I rushed past the greeters to the ladies' restroom. I re-applied my make-up in all the right spots to deflect attention from my swollen check and combed my curls to one side of my face. I then put on the glittering tiara from my conference bag.

The evening service had already started, and I followed the aisle to the front looking for the minister's section. I soon found a seat for "Reverend Cynthia Shelby" on the front row.

I did not feel like a princess, but my conference bag had crowned me like one. Regardless of how I looked or felt, He was My Heavenly Father, a King, and I was His daughter, a princess. So much so, that I had been given the best seat at the conference, because He is the King (Jehovah Ha-Melech Psalms 98:6).

Prayer

Heavenly Father, help me to always feel like the daughter of a King and give me the strength to resist what I see in the mirror, so I can focus more on what you have said about me in your Word.

Amen.

Jehovah Ha-Melech - God the King

a. Revelation 19: 16

b. Psalms 47: 6 – 7

c. John 18: 36

d. 1 Timothy 6: 13 – 15

e. Hebrews 1: 3

30

EAGLES

Peace enveloped me as I reached the top of the steps. The room was adorned with hues of gray and magenta. Chicken curry, salad greens, a variety of quiches and ginger ale spiked mimosas were the menu items chosen for the minister's luncheon.

My attention shifted to the head of one of the dining tables. I heard a mature voice tempered with experience. She cast a glow about the "upper room" intriguing us with her stories regarding heads of state, speeches to the Senate and of intimate prayer times at home.

I realized that my physical hunger had guided my feet to this current place, but Jesus had so much more waiting for me. I felt like a cadet entering a room full of accomplished military leaders. I sat among female pastors, worship leaders and other "five-fold" ministry callings. We respectfully encircled the impassioned

"general of the faith" who served as this year's conference speaker.

She spoke and we ingested His truth into our spirits.
The luncheon designed to honor female clergy had
transformed into a beautiful homily. Her words of
wisdom were like a string of pearls which had
purposely been broken so that individual pearls could
decorate our souls. My heart greedily reached for each
one as I transferred wisdom into my journal.

A balcony room directly above the sanctuary felt like
the ancient streets of Israel. We sat covered with the
residue of His presence feeling spiritually and naturally
hungry. Our gathering was both planned and spontaneous.

She spoke to us in parable-like teachings. We listened
intently to every word knowing that our time with
this prophetic voice would be short. Only the sound of
instrumental music moved about the room as
our spirits were hushed by quiet mediation.

I overheard a pastor referring to this meeting as a "gathering of eagles." I laughed within and instantly connected to this concept. I would anticipate that the eagle feels
quite different from other created birds. His presence is
bigger. God allows him to soar higher and gives him a
perspective different from most.

Similarly, the call into Christian ministry requires one serve a bigger purpose, often requir-
ing a deeper study of rudimentary scripture contexts to

embrace elevated principles of faith to share with others. Jesus designed all of us with divine purpose, especially those in Christian ministry. He teaches ministers to broaden their reach, like an eagle, so that they can affectionately soar toward Him, while grasping followers as they both recognize Jesus as the Lord Our Maker (Jehovah Hoseenu Psalms 95:6).

Prayer

Heavenly Father, help me to remember daily that you created me. You knew me in my mother's womb and have a future with a hope planned for me.

Amen.

Jehovah Hoseenu – The Lord Our Maker

a. Genesis 1:1

b. Colossians 1: 16 – 17

c. Psalms 8: 3

d. Isaiah 42: 5

e. Genesis 1: 21

31

ALL GONE

I mentioned to a friend that I desired a device which could help me track my daily steps. She offered me one she no longer used and added that she would be happy to give it to me.

Like a blessing dropped from heaven, there was a lovely gift bag waiting for me right where I sat most Sundays. I peeked in the bag with excitement and the love affair began.

That afternoon, I asked my son to synchronize my step-counter to my phone. He played with it for a while and taught me a few lessons about owning a step counting device. His teacher's instinct informed me that the device not only counted my steps, but it would report the miles that I had walked as well as the calories that I had burned. My heart fluttered with anticipation!

He went on to inform me that he would be activating

several other features that would "help" me to be a better mother as well.

"Mom, since you never remember to turn on your phone after work or meetings. I am setting your step-counter to vibrate your arm when someone calls you." I smiled smugly.

I further pondered the joys of twenty-first century motherhood. Now, I would be fully accessible to answer phone calls about why I am tardy for afternoon pickups or calls which require me to be a mediator between him and his younger sister when I am away from home.

Nevertheless, I wore my device and enjoyed checking it for steps and distance. Even the vibrating notifications were not too annoying.

One day I walked three miles at the gym and a little over a mile taking care of daily errands. I was remarkably close to achieving five miles and was just shy of my ten thousand step goal. So, I moved around in the kitchen a little longer that evening and intentionally walked up and down our stairs a couple of times, pressing toward my goal.

I checked my device again before and after showering. I allowed myself one more peek after removing my makeup and brushing my teeth. To my surprise, all my hard-earned steps were gone! Consequently, I checked my bedroom clock to learn that it was midnight and that my stockpile of numbers had vanished and now showed a clear slate for a new day!

My mind drifted into deep thought as my head eased onto my pillow. My step counting device had erased my data in preparation for a new day. The step counter was designed to show the truth just like our Heavenly Father, who is patient with His care, to bring us into the truth daily (El Emet Psalms 31:5).

Prayer

Heavenly Father, thank you that you are the God of truth.
Help me to daily read your Word, so that I my know the truth
and be free.

Amen.

El Emet – The God of Truth

a. Isaiah 65: 16

b. John 14: 6

c. John 17: 17

d. Psalms 86: 11

e. John 8: 32

32

MOTHER "SOMETIMES" KNOWS BEST

Sunday afternoons are my selected Sabbaths. Attending church service and cooking dinner are my only planned activities for the day. However, this Sunday was different because our son needed to be driven to a charity event to volunteer with his youth group.

A little persuasion, from both my husband and son, prodded me from our home to the car. I asked my son to be my co-pilot, via his cell phone, because I "thought" I lacked the navigational skills to get there.

His device and my mind began to map directions differently. He looked to his device and informed me that the next turn was to the "right" and my mother's wit, challenged that the next turn should actually be a "left."

He shook his head, at my mental mapping, and turned off his device as I routed to the location from my trusted memory. We ended up in an empty parking lot and he broke the awkward silence with, "Mom, I told you!"

I quickly turned my car around and reconnected to his suggested route, without fighting or defense. We arrived at our destination a few minutes later.

During another time, I noticed that my driver's license was soon to expire, while waiting in my son's high school carline. Now, I did "think" I remembered the location for driver's license renewal, but still asked my son, the young co-pilot to set his navigational system for the quickest route.

As usual, I followed the set route through the busy traffic, while "thinking" of a shorter route. I wanted to get there in less time than the projected fifteen minutes.

Eventually, I broke from the set path and made several "smart turns" through a nearby neighborhood to bypass the snail traffic. My son sighed and gave me a side-eyed glance. When I sensed we were close, I turned to my son and boasted, "See, it didn't take me fifteen minutes at all!"

We drove back and forth on the street where I had renewed my license, four years ago. My certainty began to wane after fifteen minutes had lapsed. It was obvious, I had left the set path and had gotten us lost once again. My son lovingly gave me a "really Mom" look and we both burst into laughter.

I apologized for asking for his help and pursuing "my own" way. The look on my son's face might be how Christ looks at us, when we seek "our own" way which typically leads us away from His desired path for our lives. He permits us to choose "our own" way and waits for us to return to Him, for recalibration because He is the Lord My Redeemer (Jehovah-Go'el Isaiah 44:22).

Prayer

Heavenly Father, help me through prayer, to follow you wholeheartedly. In the times that I stray from your path, give me the strength to recognize it, repent and recalibrate.

Amen.

Jehovah-Go'el - Lord My Redeemer

a. Psalms 19: 14

b. Job 19: 25

c. Psalms 119: 154

d. Proverbs 23: 11

e. Isaiah 41: 14

33

ENCIRCLED WITH FRIENDSHIP

An innocent pose for a birthday picture shifted my attention from the actual celebration to the friendships represented in the photo. This year's celebration was significant, because it was the first milestone birthday among my circle of close friends. One of us had stepped into a new decade of life.

Our friendships date back to the age of ten years old. I distinctly remember meeting one at church and another one while growing up in my neighborhood.

I recall meeting Toni in Sunday school where we competed in Bible games and where we shared our knowledge of biblical stories. We also sang together in both the children's and youth choirs.

I remember meeting Meridith one summer when her military parents were visiting her grandmother on my street. She was a bit younger than me, but we had the best time playing hopscotch and an assortment of games daily in my best friend's driveway.

Decades of cherished memories spilled from my soul, as I looked at the birthday picture on my phone for a second time. I remembered being warmed by those smiles before, as I nervously glanced passed them, with moistened palms on my wedding day. We repeated this scenario at the altar two other times when they both got married.

Those smiles were present again to congratulate me during both housewarmings, where they planned and prepared delicious meals for the invited guests. They genuinely shared my excitement as a new homeowner.

During the birth of my children, those smiles embraced me and my tiny new additions. Both frequently checked on me. In addition, one delivered me home catered meals and the other gift cards to ease my transition into motherhood.

I have shared a lifetime of rich celebrations and infectious smiles with them. We have celebrated graduations, new business ownership, opportunities for ministry and the birth of twins.

I mostly remember our smiles although there have been some shared tears.

Whether smiling or crying, I appreciate my close friends for being there when I needed their friendship. I must remember that my Heavenly Father is always there too,

for all my important life events. He loves us
so much, just like a good friend. The Father watches
over us and promises us that He sticks closer to us, than
a brother because He is our Friend (Reuel John 15:15).

Prayer

Heavenly Father, thank you for special friendships in my life. Help me to spend time with you daily to develop our friendship so that your promises to me may be fulfilled.

Amen.

Reuel – Friend

a. John 15: 13

b. Proverbs 18: 24

c. John 15: 14

d. James 2: 23

e. John 15: 15

34

NOTICED

My workout had been a tough one, so the thought of a warm dinner out was exciting!

My choice of seating was full of indecision. Did I want the seclusion of a cozy booth, or did I want a well-lit table spot? My eyes quickly scanned the dining room and I reluctantly settled for the table. I thought the lighting would facilitate a better date with my cell phone.

The buzz from a radiating red pager signaled me to pick up my food although my aching body delayed me. I winced through pain and pushed to the counter to get my food, when my eyes connected with a young lady seated in one of the cozy booths I had wanted. My eyes occasionally met hers as I looked up from my device from time to time. We smiled awkwardly and we both resumed eating.

Then, I sensed a presence beside me and looked up to investigate. I discovered it was the girl from the booth.

"May I take your food tray for you? I noticed you were having trouble with your knees. My Dad has had a couple of ALC (Anterior Cruciate Ligament) surgeries, and I understand how you may feel."

I agreed and thanked her. She carefully picked up the tray and disappeared. I was startled once again by her return to the table and her next request.

She seated herself across from me and asked my name and further inquired if she could pray for my knees. Again, I surrendered an innocent "yes" and she began to pray. It was kind, quick, and full of compassion.

I followed her pattern after the prayer and asked her name. I soon let Claire know that I admired her boldness. She admitted that she wanted to be obedient to the Lord's leading to pray for me and that my openness to prayer was confirmation that her leading was correct.

I reflected over the kindness in her eyes and thought about Jesus. I thought about those who encountered His kindness and experienced His compassion. Claire presented me with a unique gift. The gift of "notice" and did what I would imagine the Lord would have done. He was concerned enough to reach out to those who needed help because He is our My Helper (Jehovah Ezrah Psalms 46:1).

Prayer

Heavenly Father, help me to remember that you know me and the troubles which confront me. Thank you for being my very present help in my times of need.

Amen

Jehovah Ezrah – The Lord My Helper

a. Psalms 33: 20

b. John 14: 26

c. Hebrew 13: 6

d. John 16: 13

e. Psalms 118: 7

35

SUPREME JUDGE

Higher education cannot prepare you for everything. Like most, in college, I followed a menu of recommended courses to obtain both educational degrees and educational certificates. I was endorsed with the university's approval to communicate, teach, and administrate.

Although highly trained, I still struggled in my field of choice. My formal education fell short in teaching me how to manage all behavior, to efficiently grade papers and to decide matters as a judge would.

I quickly gathered resources from experts who had authored books on behavior and located rubrics to assist me with grading. However, the craft of executing sound judgment came only over time.

My "newness" to the classroom made me an easy target for a "sob" story. Tearful, wide-eyed confessions twisted my heart until I encountered conflicting accounts about the same incident.

Suspicions led me to question both children separately, because I knew that they both could not be "right." I came to a solid verdict after examining, cross examining, and calling in a few expert witnesses. I learned to politely listen to all suspects, with my ears and not my heart.

My "judicial skills" were put to the test once again when I became the mother of more than one child. Tearful, wide eyes were a little harder to resist this time because they were now my own flesh and blood.

Nevertheless, when the time came, I executed my line of questioning fairly for both the plaintiff and the defendant. In love, I listened and litigated each sibling rivalry case to justice.

Teaching and "mothering" have made me more discerning about all matters from "borrowed" pencils to who was in the bathroom first. Over time, the deliveries of my judgments have been perfected into calm and collected discourses.

I am often reminded of the nature of my Heavenly Father's love toward me when dealing with students or my own children. He is tender with me when circumstances and when evidence is not stacked in my favor.

He listens with compassion to my prayerful testimony and allows me to experience both His love and peace. I am comforted knowing that He can listen without judgment because He alone is the Judge (Shaphat Genesis 18:25).

Prayer

Heavenly Father, help me to remember that I am accountable to you daily. Allow me to be comforted in knowing that you listen without judgment and are quick to forgive me.

Amen.

Shaphat – Judge

a. Psalms 139: 13 – 16

b. John 3: 16

c. Job 33: 4

d. Romans 6: 23

e. Psalms 75: 7

36

JUST PERFECT

A recent health scare, during a wellness visit, motivated me to re-gain perspective about my own health and life.

I instantly aligned myself with nutritional information to make changes and to talk my family into obtaining gym memberships with me. Creating time to exercise, for this wife and mother, felt a little selfish at first to exclusively focus on my own self-care.

This year, holidays like Halloween, Thanksgiving, Christmas, and my birthday were celebrated with slight dietary modifications. I aligned myself to "sacrifice" both at the table and at the gym.

I reprioritized my schedule, made decisions with intention and learned to say "no" to myself.

I was elated about my weight loss on the scale each week. I also enjoyed the "non scale" victories, like how my clothes fit. However, I still contended with the image I saw in the mirror.

Honestly, my eyes had much to celebrate regarding the noticeable change in my face, arms, legs, and breasts. I had lost enough weight to improve my health, but still lacked satisfaction.

Amidst celebration, I was somehow unable to celebrate my mid-section although it had decreased in size, too. My eyes always seem to zero in on the imperfections of my stomach. My body still possessed the contour of the two blessings that I carried for nine months.

I know that perceptions through a looking glass are subject to that of the perceiver. I have learned that it is not the mirror which determines who is fairest, but it is me. The beauty beheld in my life comes from my eyes alone. Further thoughts brought me to a solid conclusion about my private quest for body perfection. My body was the compilation of the circle of women who have preceded me in my family and a little bit of my own doing as well.

After thinking about my body, I realized a deeper revelation. My body was given to me from the Father God to fulfill my unique purpose on the earth. I am expected to keep it healthy for His service and not mediate on its imperfections. My feelings should be centered upon Him because God is My Exceeding Joy (El Simchah Giyli Psalms 43:4).

Prayer

Heavenly Father, help me to accept the beauty that you provide for me in life without expecting other people, things, or myself to be perfect because perfection can only be found in you Help me to focus on all the joys and not the negatives in life.

Amen.

El Simchah Giyli – My Exceeding Joy

a. Nehemiah 8: 10

b. Psalm 16: 11

c. Romans 14: 17

d. John 16: 24

e. Romans 12: 2

37

FORGET ME NOTS

Attending school and working in schools most of my life has exposed me to an array of educational philosophies. Teachers are regularly expected to keep a mental record of both positive and negative directives made toward students.

For instance, best practice would dictate that for every negative comment, three positive comments are needed to offset the negativity, so that the brain gravitates to the positive versus the negative. I tend to be a positive person but have found myself gravitating toward the negative in my mind.

Most people take pleasure in the beauty of snow. I most certainly do too, but a snow-covered road triggers my thoughts back to an accident from an unpredicted snow and ice storm. I over corrected, on black ice, hit a truck head on, and it crashed me into a tree. It has been close to nineteen years now and my mind still produces that flashback when I drive on that same road.

I get compliments frequently about my skin, but my eyes tend to notice the scars from the results of an accident at my grandmother's home. I am told that I was playing near a vintage furnace in the bathroom. The healed burn on the inside of my forearms documents the unexpected fall and causes me not to forget.

During my morning brushes, it would be quite natural for me to focus only on my teeth and the task at hand. However, I see the bare spaces where my four wisdom teeth once grew. Four extractions in one day left my checks swollen and my gums in trauma for a week. My mind reverts to that time, of my youth, whenever my tongue or my toothbrush explores those empty places.

I am most grateful for a healthy body, but instead of admiring my best features, I find myself noticing imperfections like the stretch marks on my stomach, from my two gifts from God. After pregnancy my congestion cleared up, my legs released their swelling but, my body kept several tiny keepsake markings that my eyes frequently notice.

While my mind may focus on the negative, the mind of Christ operates much differently. I can freely go to Him in prayer to confess acts of sin and to ask for forgiveness. He forgives me without any remembrance of the wrong I have committed. He absolutely forgets the negativity of sins and receives us with forgiveness because He is the Lord of Forgiveness (Eloah Selikhot Nehemiah 9:17).

Prayer

Heavenly Father, thank you for being a forgiving God who can listen to my shortcomings and forgives me without judgment. Help me to come to you daily with a forgiving heart and with forgiveness for those who have offended me.

Amen.

'Eloah Selikhot - God of Forgiveness

a. Matthew 6: 14 – 15

b. Ephesians 4: 31 – 32

c. 1 John 1: 9

d. Daniel 9: 9

e. Mark 11: 25

38

WHEN GOD IS ALL YOU REALLY NEED

Strange, my text message was unable to go through. After several failed attempts, I stopped texting and prayed that my son Stan would look for me in my usual place in the car line after school.

Soon, I was greeted by Stan's smiling face and quickly headed toward home. Things could not be better for this teacher. No after-school faculty meeting, a quick student pick-up line, and now I was heading home to enjoy a relaxing evening.

A letter from my cell phone service provider beckoned me from the kitchen counter. I could feel the peaceful calm beginning to seep from my body, as I learned that my payment was overdue. What? Overdue?

How can it be overdue when I never received the original bill? I read the strong tones of the letter several times before I called the customer service number at the bottom of the page. My current peace had all but evaporated as I listened to the repetitious hold music and explained my current situation to a series of people who struggled to understand my need. I gave up on the idea of a homemade dinner. I headed out to solve the cell phone issue locally.

Taking a deep breath, I pulled into the parking lot of my service provider. A young man, who looked my son's age, was nice and informed me that I could not pay my bill with a check. I learned that they had stopped accepting payment like that, three months ago. I reluctantly reached for my credit card and walked with him to an automated machine.

I spilled from the store exhausted from the day and was unsettled by a range of emotions which had surged through my body in such a short amount of time. I stood beyond the store gazing into the window of a popular coffee shop and thought, "A cookie is just what I need right NOW."

My mind downloaded the events of the day as my cookie was being bagged. I recalled the "happiness" I felt to have arrived early in the pick-up line, the "confusion" I experienced when my cell phone would not text, the "shock" regarding the overdue bill, the "inconvenience" I felt when I could not pay the way I desired, the "frustration" I felt when I could not get the help I needed via my land line and the "exhaustion" I felt after everything was over.

I needed the comfort of my Father God and not that of a shortbread cookie. It is His presence which truly satisfies. I wonder how differently this day would have ended, if I had just reached out to God to both help and to comfort me. He is the All Sufficient One who can handle any problem or disappointment that I may experience (El Shaddi Genesis 17: 1-2).

Prayer

Heavenly Father, help me to talk to you about the needs I have in my life and keep me from reaching toward other things for the satisfaction that only you can give.

Amen.

El Shaddi – The All Sufficient One

a. 2 Corinthians 2: 12

b. 2 Timothy 3: 15 – 17

c. Philippians 1: 20

d. 2 Corinthians 12: 9

e. James 1: 2 – 4

39

DETERMINED

Sometimes determination trumps protocol. I was the baby in the family and that birth order afforded me to be spoiled and made the inclination of being gutsy quite safe.

I grew quicker emotionally than I did physically. I always knew what I wanted and had a natural determination how to get it. Admittedly, my set temperament did get me into trouble from time to time.

My mother was quite determined too. She stayed committed to teaching Sunday school, after my birth, being her fifth child. She took me with her each Sunday to instruct the young adults.

In an uncommon shift, I went from the young adult class to the preschool class. My exposure to the scriptures at an early age helped me to connect to the fundamentals of the faith quickly. I understood biblical concepts as a young girl.

One Sunday morning, I found myself stirring to action over a sequence of Sunday school lessons. My heart was challenged to think about eternity although I was just a five-year-old. I felt a pull within my heart to do something about what I had heard in Sunday school.

We always arrived early for service since we were already at church for Sunday school. My mom would bring me a snack and would provide her lap for a nap during service. This Sunday, I asked her to wake me up for the baptismal portion of the service.

However, I woke up on my own to see the pastor dressed in a white robe baptizing people. I was upset about not being awakened, because I had planned to give my heart to Christ that Sunday.

I was still determined to execute my plan and I discussed my discontent with my mother. She took me by the hand and walked me down the aisle to the front of the church. Every eye shifted from the baptism to us at the front of the church which was not the normal protocol.

Our pastor left the baptismal and met us at the altar. He kindly asked me what I wanted, and I gave him a heartfelt confession of faith and let him know that I wanted to be a child of God that day. He prayed with me the sinner's prayer and sent me to get dressed for baptism.

My baptism memory reminds me of how determined I was to have Christ as my Savior. I wanted what I had learned from the scriptures to be a part of my life. I was determined for Christ to be my Lord because He is the God Who Saves (El Moshaah Psalms 68:20).

Prayer

Heavenly Father, thank you for saving me and giving me a new life through your Son Jesus Christ. I pray that I will continue to be determined to know you better each day.

Amen.

El Moshaah – The God Who Saves Psalms

a. Romans 5: 8

b. 1 John 2: 2

c. Habakkuk 3: 18

d. Acts 11:4

e. Acts 2: 21

~SUMMER~

Song of Solomon 2:12
The flowers appear on the earth;
The time of singing has come,
And the voice of the turtledove
Is heard in our land.

40

LESSONS AT THE BEACH

My husband helped me settle into a comfortable beach spot complete with my umbrella, drinks, and a book to read. Watching my family enjoy the beach is my ideal beach experience, because I am more inclined to rest and relax.

Both children followed my husband down a sandy path to play. I had planned to read or to sleep. Somehow, I became so distracted by my surroundings that I decided to saunter down the beach to locate my family.

I soon discovered that the children were playing water games with their dad in the ocean. My daughter was inching into the deep waters and when the waves increased, she would shout, "Get me d-a-d-d-y!" My husband, who stood in proximity, would scoop her up and together they would laugh.

My son joined them, and the game play evolved into "Sharks and Piranhas." Both children would wade toward their dad, but the strength of the waves would cause them to retreat and to pursue him once again. Each time they went further into the water to be near him as he watched them with undivided attention.

I, too, became entrapped by the water's spell and eventually stepped into the warm rush of foam. I studied the wave patterns and planted my feet solidly on the ocean floor. When I saw big waves approaching in the distance, I braced myself to make my stance immoveable.

This water game was repeated and again. Each time I sought better footing to stand strong for a longer length of time. The Lord began to teach me in His outdoor classroom.

My children's water play focused on their dad. They love their daddy and enjoy spending time with him. I was reminded that our Heavenly Father really does need to be the center of our lives. We should always seek the Lord's safety and security.

Our Father loves it when we call out to Him and jump in His arms when things get too rough in our lives. I realized that day that it is okay to still need our heavenly Daddy. We really cannot do life all by ourselves and should not attempt to try.

My own water play reminded me that when I refuse to be distracted by the wave of daily cares and I anchor my feet upon what is steady, which is Jesus our Lord, I will not be so easily moved by the waves that life can sometimes produce.

I must seek Him daily in prayer and I must keep Him as the center of my focus, because He is the Lord who is my Strength in Trouble (Jehovah-'Uzam Psalms 46: 1 – 3).

Prayer

Heavenly Father, steady my feet in your word today, so that I may remain steady and overcome the adversities which crash into my life.

Amen.

Jehovah-'Uzam – The Lord Strength in Trouble

a. Psalms 27: 5

b. Psalms 138: 7

c. Psalms 50: 15

d. Psalms 91: 15

e. Psalms 46: 1

41

FROM MASTERPIECE TO MASTER
PLEASE HELP

Our friends had invited us to a dinner party, so I arose early to start preparing a Pineapple Upside Down Cake. I added and blended all the ingredients with great care and anticipation. I was planning a "masterpiece" for dessert, to be shared with friends.

I added a few personal touches and decided to bake it in a metal Bundt pan although I had countless successes with my glass pan in the past. My thought was to do something different this morning.

Once it was placed in the oven, I walked around the kitchen cleaning and straightening a bit. I peeked at my "masterpiece" from time to time through the tiny oven window.

Soon the timer signaled to me   it was ready. The smell was H-E-A-V-E-N-L-Y! My mother had taught me a cake cooling technique that worked well, but I never really liked how gumminess formed between the plate and the cake. So, today I had a different idea. I would gently place my "masterpiece" onto the cooling rack I used when baking cookies, to avoid the cake bottom goo.

I gently placed the cake onto the rack and immediately, it began to break apart! As the pieces released themselves from the mold's shape, they produced tiny wisps of steam. I thought, "What kind of "masterpiece" is this?

I decided to slice the cake into pieces to hide the fact that it had totally fallen apart. I selected a beautiful plate and arranged it in an attractive pattern. I was still very committed to the "masterpiece idea" although my process had not been ideal.

In years past, I would have made another dessert or would have just picked up something "perfect" from the store on the way. However, this time I was taking my plate full of Pineapple Upside Down pieces to our dinner date. I realized that I had grown a bit. I was unbothered by its appearance, for I was sure it would taste good and that is what really matters.

After dinner, I unveiled my "masterpieces," topped them with vanilla bean ice cream and enjoyed my labor of love along with the others. It was quite tasty, and God strengthened my heart through this experience and taught me an important lesson in the process.

My "masterpiece" did not look like what I had envisioned, but it was "just right" for the occasion. When our lives do not go as we expect, we must trust our process in the hands of our Masterful God. He takes the broken pieces of our journey and crafts them into something beautiful, for the world to see and taste because He is Masterful (Adoni Jeremiah 32:17).

Prayer

Heavenly Father, give me grace to handle the broken pieces in my life and help me to regularly submit each piece to you because you make all things beautiful in your time.

Amen.

Adoni – The Lord Master

a. Isaiah 9: 6

b. 1 Samuel 24: 4 – 8

c. Isaiah 10: 16

d. Psalms 8: 1

e. Psalms 103: 19

42

CHILDHOOD IMPRINTS

As a child, I could not help but to notice how much my parents loved taking care of the yard. My dad would mow the lawn and trim the hedges while my mom would plant the flowers and keep everything well-watered.

Both Mom and Dad adhered to my grandmother's fixed flower rule. Granny believed that you should wait until after the first of May to plant your treasures in the ground.

As an adult, I aimed to continue the tradition of planting flowers in early May. Unlike my mom, I consistently worked full-time outside of my home and had little energy to work in the yard after teaching all day.

I searched for creative ways to meet their "unspoken" expectations and demands within my head. I frequently hired neighbors to assist me with the task of gardening or forced myself to put in another day's work after my job.

I have discovered that the routines, modeled before me as a child, have left imprints on my adult behavior.

Dusting on Saturdays was my regular chore when I lived at home. Week in and week out, I would wipe down and reposition each "what-not." I dry dusted some surfaces and used furniture polish for others. A few Saturdays pass without me thinking about dusting, although it is fresh in my mind.

Similarly, immediately after Sunday service, I was expected to take off my Sunday clothes before playing or doing anything else. My parents generated a modest income and wanted me to learn how to take care of what I had. My husband and I earn more than my parents, but we still require our children to remove their Sunday best once they are home from church.

My mom was a mastermind when it came to celebrating birthdays, her intimate parties were the best. In our home, I celebrate birthdays just as I did when I grew up. My children make their requests for themed parties' months in advance, and I strive to make each one special!

I have learned repeated exposure to family traditions can imprint certain vales into our hearts. Similarly, daily exposures to scriptures are intended to imprint

biblical values within our spirits. Christ's imprint upon
our spirts shows us what we should know and how
to grow, because He is a good Father and our
Maker (O'saynu Psalm 95:6).

Prayer

Heavenly Father, help me to remember that you are my Maker and help to model my life's steps according to the imprints of your scripture in my heart.

Amen.

O' Saynu – The Lord Our Maker

a. Psalms 100: 3

b. Nehemiah 9: 6

c. Genesis 1: 1

d. Isaiah 45: 7

e. Ephesians 3: 9

43

UNSEEN BLESSINGS

One evening, I noticed that my children were crafting something on the computer. I became curious and inquired about their intense focus. My daughter raised a piece of notebook paper in the air and informed me that she was starting her own business for the summer.

Her business plan was inspired by her desire to own her own electronic device. She calculated that an enterprise of dog walking, plant-watering, and caring for toddlers would get her within reach of her goal by December.

As a new business manager, she contracted her brother to do design work, recruited me to get the flyers printed and enlisted the help of her dad with distribution. As her mom, I labored without fee, but was generously compensated by her gutsy determination and by her incredible vision.

Money began to flow her way as she executed solid business steps. To expedite her savings, she also moonlighted by offering additional services for "pay" around the house. She eagerly loaded as well as unloaded the dishwasher, swept the sidewalk after grass cuttings, and organized my teacher files.

All monies were funneled into her savings other than her Sunday tithes and offerings. She conveniently left her money "at home" when we went out to eat or to shop. I believe those forgetful practices were a part of her money-saving strategy.

In the giving spirit of Christmas, we bought her the electronic device she had been saving for all summer and fall. I did not spoil the surprise but encouraged her to continue to save and to be a good steward with her money.

It was difficult to watch her work so hard for something I secretly knew she already had. However, I allowed her to continue her efforts, because I had the "perfect" life lesson in mind.

We visited my dad's home on Christmas Eve for fellowship, for gift exchange and for our traditional holiday meal. My daughter held a different type of excitement that evening. Her granddad's generous Christmas gift was a blessing and put her just shy of her set goal.

I was reminded of a simple truth while watching my daughter mastermind her enterprise to save over one hundred dollars. Christ purchased salvation thousands of years ago, so that I would enjoy eternal life with Him. He patiently watches for us to learn of the blessing that He has already purchased for us because He is our loving Savior (Jehovah-Yasha Luke 2:11).

Prayer

Heavenly Father, help me to discover all your unique blessings for me. Show me how to share with others your most important blessing, which is the precious gift of salvation, so that they may experience eternity with you.

Amen.

Jehovah Yasha – The Lord Our Savior

a. Isaiah 45: 21 – 22

b. 2 Samuel 22: 1 – 3

c. Luke 1: 47

d. 1 John 4: 14

e. Acts 13: 23

44

ANTICIPATION

Maturity can be an intriguing process. My desire for certain foods has both increased and decreased. I now smile pleasantly and speak with unguarded honesty where I would not have before, and I also cherish the people in my life so much more.

As a child everything was so exciting! Christmas, birthdays, snow days and summer vacations lured me through the year. There was always something to look forward to, and my ability to anticipate was young and vibrant.

The mental energy required to be an adult tends to deplete the stores for expectation and anticipation. Committing to memory the rotation of carpools, daily meetings and hectic schedules leaves little room for energetic thinking.

Recently, I tapped back into the fountain of youthful anticipation! I was given a device to track my physical movement. I wore it so faithfully that it began to fall apart. A close friend shared that she had once contacted the company and she was mailed a replacement immediately.

Something inside began to stir within me at the sound of that news!

I called the company the next day! The polite customer service representative was refreshing, unlike some experiences I have had with other companies.

The next day, I felt a rush of excitement when there was an email waiting for me about my device! I was asked about my experience and was given the expected date of arrival. In addition, I was issued an order number which would allow me to track the movement of my device from the company to my house.

Waves of anticipation began to brighten the daily mundane and I looked forward to the arrival of my new device. I found myself checking my email to read about the capabilities of my new step-counter and to learn of its daily journey to my home.

Finally, the day of arrival! Surprisingly, I enjoyed the anticipation over something so small. This experience reminded me that I should get excited about the daily blessings from the Lord. I should never take anything for granted and should have anticipation for all His biblical promises. The anticipation of receiving each blessing, for ourselves and others, should excite us because He is the Faithful God (El Emunah Deuteronomy 7:9).

Prayer

Heavenly Father, thank you for giving me life. Help me remember that you have so many blessings in store for my life and help me to both anticipate as well as to expect your goodness daily.

Amen.

El Emunah – Faithful God

a. Deuteronomy 7: 9

b. 1 Corinthians 1: 9

c. 2 Thessalonians 3: 3

d. Hebrews 10: 13

e. 1 Corinthians 10: 13

45

LIQUID GOLD

As a new mom, attempting to do everything right was my goal, although I carried a certain amount of "mommy guilt" because things did not always go right. It was a daily challenge to drink the required amount of water and to eat balanced meals while taking care of a newborn.

Motherhood was new, but I was becoming a bit more instinctive about a few tasks such learning to express and store my milk. Like any production manager, I kept a watchful eye on my supply.

I could not resist inventorying my precious stockpiles of milk in between naps and caring for my daughter. My prized possessions were stored in tiny bags in our "freezer-safe." Each one was dated and showed varied amounts of expressed mother's love. They were just beautiful to behold!

Today, I had planned an afternoon excursion to buy some diapers and a cute outfit for my tiny princess. I was completely excited and fantasized about "baby-free" adventures like this! In preparation, I developed a care list for Dad. I fed as well as changed her in record time to leave the house.

On my way out of the door, I briefed my husband that she was well fed and that I would be home again before her next feeding.

He smiled in his usual way and assured me that he had everything under control. It was different seeing my bundle of joy with him in the man cave, but mom had things to do. This girl was set for a little fun and f-r-e-e-d-o-m!

I timed my shopping spree down to the second and arrived home a few minutes ahead of schedule. Yes! I opened the door and could not believe my eyes.

My gaze should have landed on the two of them inter-acting so sweetly on the couch, but all I could see was the half-used bottle of "liquid gold" on the coffee table. I felt faint and my breathing became rushed and anxious now that my arduous work was wasted. I distinctly remember telling him that she would not need a feeding until I returned home.

In that moment, I headed toward the kitchen to see if anymore "bags of gold" had been stolen from the freezer safe. The cool air calmed my anger and helped me to refocus. I thought, my daughter and I are both God's creation and He had equipped me to be a mother in this season of my life. I realized that I needed to put more trust in God's provision and not in my own ability to produce the needed milk. I needed to look at Him as my Provider (Jehovah Jireh Genesis 22:14).

Prayer

Heavenly Father, help me to remember that you are God who supplies all my needs. I know Lord that I am able, but you make all things possible.

Amen.

Jehovah Jireh – The Lord Will Provide

a. Genesis 22: 13 – 14

b. Psalms 107: 9

c. Matthew 15: 32 – 38

d. Deuteronomy 2: 7

e. Matthew 6: 31

46

RIGHT STANDING

To keep growing adolescents well-fed and clothed is a continuous job for any mother. When my children were younger, I labored to keep their bibs and play outfits in mint condition. I knew the value of gently worn clothing, because my mother taught me the art of consigning well before it was the "chic mommy" thing to do. My inspections, of my children's clothing, were worthy of white glove tests and I was always well compensated for my re-sale items.

Now, their arms, legs and feet are a growing challenge in more than one way. I shop to replace their wardrobes as quickly as the seasons change.

My love for shopping, couponing and searching for bargains makes the process easier, although it is ongoing. I defer to my husband's wisdom to choose our son's attire, while I assume the task of styling fashions for our daughter.

I routinely scan closets and storage tubs for clothing they have outgrown. To my dismay, I find some outfits which appear to be worn only once and even outfits with tags still attached. I have a sorting process which stems from my baby consignment days. Overly worn items are discarded and new or gently used items are subject to be donated as well as resold.

One afternoon, I became concerned with my findings as I attempted to purge my daughter's closet. I presented my concern to our young princess. She quickly shared that she had completely forgotten that she had those items of clothing.

I thought more about our conversation as I walked away. I rarely forget the purchases I have made. Typically, I was the one who invested time to obtain them, or I was the one who budgeted to pay for them. So, it makes sense that I remember my purchases, because they personally cost me something and my children do not remember, because it costs them nothing.

My right standing with God was purchased by His son Jesus Christ. I was never required to hang on a cross or to shed blood to pay for the sins of humankind. My reflective thoughts helped me to equate my daughter's closet to my right standing with Jesus Christ.

Christ's sacrifice, on the cross, paid my debt of sin in full. When I received Christ into my heart, through prayer, I gained access to a lifestyle free of guilt and sin.

I, too, act as though I have forgotten what He has purchased for me when I condemn myself for sinful acts. It is through prayerful repentance that I exchange my sin for His righteousness, because He alone is The Lord Our Righteousness (Jehovah Tsidkenu Jeremiah 23:6)

Prayer

Heavenly Father, thank you for the ultimate sacrifice you made for me. Help me to remember what you have purchased for me at the cross.

Amen.

Jehovah Tsidkenu – The Lord Our Righteous

a. Isaiah 51: 5

b. Romans 1: 17

c. Psalms 89: 16

d. Philippians 3: 9

e. Jeremiah 23: 6

47

WHILE I WAIT

Since Mom's passing, eleven years ago, I have become more attentive to dad's needs. Attending vision exams, helping him with things around his home and sometimes accompanying him to church have all become an important priority.

My late sister typically visits "the family" church with Dad on special occasions, however, this year was my turn.

Service was just as I had remembered. There were plenty of warm hugs, inquiries about my siblings, familiar songs, and a great morning message. Emotionally, I regressed to the thoughts and feelings of my youth, and it felt like I was home again.

After service, I followed my dad down the steps to the fellowship hall for dinner. Although we were seated first, to my surprise, we were not served first.

Initially, the "wait" provided us with time to compare our thoughts about the message and for me to reconnect with former church members and friends.

The passing of each food tray released aromas which heightened my hunger and eventually began to annoy me. My external smiles and laughter suppressed my internal feelings of frustration. I thought, "Cynthia, you really can't change the order in which you are served, so calm down and occupy yourself." I refocused myself to reach for the positive.

To self soothe, I looked back at the program to review my sermon notes, made the hospitality manager aware of Dad's dietary needs and chatted with an extremely sweet little girl who happened by our table.

I realized that there is a ridiculously small percentage of what we can control in life while waiting for some things to "change." It is in those moments that we must redirect our focus to the positive versus the negative.

I could have chosen to meditate on the lack of immediate service and become irritated about having to wait, but that would not have made our meals show up any quicker. Spending quality time with Dad in the church of my childhood was the best "feast" set before me in that moment.

I am personally thankful that our relationship with the Lord is not a long delay. We never have to wait for His presence nor for Him to show up, because He is always with us (Jehovah Shammah Deuteronomy 31:6).

Prayer

Heavenly Father, help me to stay positive during seasons of waiting. Give me a heart to focus on you, to take care of others and to keep my own emotions intact. I trust your plan for me and will wait for the direction you have purposed for me.

Amen.

Jehovah Shammah – The Lord Is There

a. Genesis 27: 6 – 8

b. Exodus 33: 18 – 20

c. 1 Samuel 2:21

d. 2 Kings 13: 22 – 23

e. 1 Chronicles 29: 10 – 11

48

INVISIBLE GOALS

My internal navigation system assists me in reaching milestones year after year. I do not recall if my driving thoughts came from me or from someplace else. Nevertheless, I felt "the push."

An early goal of mine was to become a teenager although most would agree it had little to do with planning and more to do with biology. I could not wait to thrust through the doorway of womanhood and its unforeseen complications. I relished the thought of styling my own outfits and styling my own hair.

My sweet sixteenth birthday was the next pressing goal, on the road to maturity. I just wanted to take hold of any set of keys at this age, so I could accelerate beyond the reach of my parents to obtain my first job and to chauffeur my friends to school and back.

I had a focused goal of meeting "Mr. Right" and to fall in love. Higher education consumed the bulk of my twenties and slowed my ticking clock, although getting married stayed on my radar. I did not want to marry too late in life, because I wanted to be an active young mother.

I accomplished the goal of marriage, although I arrived at the altar well after "my" intended time. I was prepared to bask in the joys of being a newlywed, in our cozy one-bedroom apartment, but that did not happen. My brain projected forward to remind me that future children will need a home and space to play, so the search began for the perfect house.

My "clock", which I had pacified in my twenties, was progressing rapidly at this point. I realized that any delay could compromise the "dream" of birthing my own family. So, we planned, pursued, and pushed toward that goal.

Calculating the appropriate spacing between children became my next undertaking, after my first pregnancy and delivery were complete.
Researching suggested that two to three years apart would be optimal for sibling connection and for making college tuition more affordable. I was enjoying my young family, although I had concerns about their futures filed away in my brain.

Now, thoughts for college planning were in overdrive. The blessings of long legs, technological know-how and left-handedness were now viewed as marketable skills, worthy of scholarships.

Admittedly, I have struggled to balance my Christian upbringing to trust the Lord with constant goal setting and planning. The Lord shields me from my hypersensitivity to meeting goals which often takes my eyes off Him. It is in quiet times of reflection, that I am reminded that the Lord has a specific plan for my life, and He can shield me from the stress of my own planning (Jehovah Magen Deuteronomy 33:29).

Prayer

Heavenly Father, thank you for being the brightest light in this darkened world. Help me to remember that your Word should be the only lamp to guide my feet toward the life in which you have planned for me.

Amen.

Jehovah Magen – The Lord My Shield

a. Genesis 15: 1

b. Psalm 115: 9

c. Proverbs 30: 5

d. Psalm 33: 20

e. Psalm 3: 3

49

THE BATTLE OF CHAMPIONS

I decided to join the excitement across the globe as my household lay asleep here in the Western Hemisphere. It is common for me to be awake before my family and even before the rise of the sun, but it is uncommon for me to turn on the television.

Silently I wrote as the white noise of athletic shoes screeched back and forth across a tennis court. Eruptions from cheering fans caused my attention to shift from my computer to my television periodically.

It was the last day of the tournament and the final match between two champions. The stretch of three hours and some minutes found the players in the bottom of the fifth match hungrier than ever and full of fervor. They positioned their rackets like fencing swords and played clashing with strength.

At times it looked like David and Goliath as the seventeenth seed legitimately battled the ninth seed. They fought, like the champions they were, as the final minutes faded into intense commentary from the broadcasters.

I stopped writing and was fully engaged at this point. The final serve was challenged so I waited, in a frozen position, for the official call. Somehow, my heart began to release empathy for the runner up, because I knew there could only be one winner.

Once the winner was announced, the crowd erupted as the winner stood in disbelief. He then fell to the ground completely overwhelmed. His opponent held back emotion as he retreated to the sideline to change his shirt and to prepare for the awards ceremony.

Both were congratulated and received awards after a string of pleasantries and the recognition of tournament sponsors. Each champion was permitted to address the standing, sold-out crowd.

I was pressed beyond normal emotion as they each graciously shifted attention from themselves to the fans, to the sponsors and then to each other. They wrapped their words eloquently in humility as one conceded loss and the other shared how they had both won. Something about their selflessness, decorum and grace made me emotional.

The two competitors caused me to think about the heart of Father God. He is not a harsh God but One who is full of compassion. He understands the battles we endure in life and is always available to help us right where we are because He is a Compassionate/ Merciful God (El Rachum Deuteronomy 4:31).

Prayer

Heavenly Father, help me to remember that your compassion and tender mercies are new every morning. Cover me with your mercy when I need it the most.

Amen.

El Rachum - The God of Compassion / Merciful God

a. Deuteronomy 7: 9

b. 2 Samuel 22: 26

c. Mark 6: 34

d. Hebrews 4: 16

e. Ephesians 2: 4 – 5

50

THE ECONOMY OF MOTHERS

Seven years of my career have been dedicated to solely educating boys. Mothers of boys are a unique sect in the "economy of mothers." They can be especially protective as they adore and navigate their young cubs.

I have been that "protective mom" at times, too, as well as many other "types" of mothers in my search to be the best parent.

While mothering infants, I memorized the best portions of well-known baby books to ensure that my children were rolling, crawling, cruising, and walking at the targeted ages. I was also attentive to their educational readiness for school, being their first teacher.

Once they started school, I was the standard "helicopter mom" who always wanted to be "there." I lingered at drop offs and volunteered as often as I could, although my "working mom" status, kept me from ever being the coveted "homeroom mom."

Somewhere along the way I bought into the idea of raising prodigy children. I became the "grandstand mom" and the "stage mom." My athlete husband deemed it necessary for us to get our son acclimated to league play, so I became that mom. Also, being a strong advocate for the arts, I decided our daughter should experience dance, so I coached her through each dance performance and coached the voice inflections for her stage performances.

Ultimately, I transitioned into the "talent scout mom" during their middle school years as I evaluated their giftings. I shuttled them from school, to practice and to drive through dinners. I surveyed their talents to fit them with the correct instruments, the correct athletic teams, and the correct after-school clubs.

Honestly, the "college recruiter mom" felt the most natural to me since I was a trained educator. I frequently studied course offerings and I frequently kept a watchful eye on their grade point averages. I taxied them to study groups, to college entrance exams and to college visits.

I worked diligently, to balance the status of the "church mom" throughout every other mothering phase. I have been the mom who has helped them to memorize Bible verses, to participate in children's choirs and to attend vacation bible school in the summers. It was innate for me to share biblical principles with them, as I taught them to share their toys, to pray over their meals, and offer thanks to God before going to bed.

Truthfully, all I ever needed to be is the "Spirit-led mom" who teaches and trains her children in the way they should go. I am promised that when they are old, those teachings will not depart from them. The Lord lovingly watches over us, as His created children. I lovingly watch over my own children, as the Father watches over us with parental compassion to ensure that we arrive at destiny on time because He is the One who knows everything about us as the Omniscient God (El De'ot John 21:17).

Prayer

Heavenly Father, help me to be a mom who is led by your Spirit only. Help me to train the children you have entrusted to me in the scriptures and in the way they should go.

Amen.

El De'ot – The God of Knowledge

a. Psalms 139: 1 – 6

b. 1 Samuel 2:3

c. 1 John 3: 30

d. 1 Kings 8: 39

e. Matthew 10: 29 – 30

51

LOOK AWAY

I quickly exited onto a turnpike with full intent to have some professional copies made before a routine meeting.

In the distance, I saw a man with a tattered cardboard sign. I did not know the circumstances behind his sign, nor did I know what it was requesting.

The light turned red in the distance, and I mentally began to calculate where my vehicle would stop. Just as I had thought, my ceased motion would bring me face to face with the man and his cardboard sign.

Now, I was close enough to see a bit of his back story which was communicated with faded military fatigues and what looked to be a well-traveled duffle bag. My eyes shifted down as I pretended to search for something in my car and then to check messages on my cell phone. I lacked the courage to look him in the face.

I sighed with relief once the light changed to green, allowing me to escape my current situation. The humanity, born from my Christian upbringing, would not let me discard this experience.

My heart wanted to investigate why I looked away from his cardboard cares. My reaction to the cardboard sign was like the emotions I feel when I switch the channel away from commercials about starving children or neglected animals.

The recurring thoughts shrouded me like a burial wrapping, as I plowed through my day, causing me to seek resolve by the end of the day.

Honestly, I looked away because I felt overwhelmed with the sight of great need and redirected my focus to ease my own pain. Sometimes I look away because I cannot tell if the need is authentic or fake. Sometimes I look away because I am concerned about my own safety.

Momentarily, I am sympathetic but lack the courage to help. When the need is too great, I find me doing nothing at all.

Thankfully, our Father God does not look away from us as we flash signs of distress to Him in the roller coaster seasons of our lives. He is a God who understands our weaknesses and shortcomings. Our God never looks away from us and I can take comfort that He is the God who always sees me (El Roi Genesis 16:1).

Prayer

Heavenly Father, thank you that you are known as the God who sees me. I pray that your Spirit will help me see others as you do and that you would show me how to help those in genuine need.

Amen.

El Roi – The God Who Sees Me

a. Genesis 16: 13 – 14

b. 2 Chronicles 16: 9

c. Psalms 15: 3

d. Matthew 6: 3 – 4

e. Psalms 121: 3 – 8

52

THE BUSY BURDEN

I had already forgotten the calm which came from July's vacation, and the memory of early August had faded into a blur with my preparation for school. Encountering the onset of fast-paced days caused my mind to drift back to the "happy places" of summer where I felt excellent but stayed very "busy."

"Busy" was good for me. "Busy" purged our home from unwanted and underutilized items. "Busy" was the reward I enjoyed when morning exercise was over. "Busy" helped me to find sweet deals on everything from dishware to name brand tennis shoes. "Busy" made it possible to stay in contact with my elderly dad, sneak in lunch dates with my sister and regularly chat with friends on social media. Things were good until "busy" followed me into my quiet time one summer morning and everything changed.

I physically sat with my Bible and daily devotional but with a million "busy" ideas and thoughts which
stood as a barrier to His presence. After contending for
my focus, I was then able to spend time with the
Lord. There was a familiar scripture, which appeared
on the home page of my Bible app. It read,
"Be still and know that I am God. I will be exalted among the heathen; I will be exalted in the earth
(Psalms 46:10)." I smiled within, thinking what
a strange coincidence.

Eventually, I proceeded to my devotional passage for
the day and discovered that the scripture reference for
the day was Psalms 46:10. By this time, my internal
smile had faded away. I ingested the repeti-
tion of truth. I repented in prayer for embracing
"busy," relying on "busy," and allowing "busy" to
distract me away from His leadings as well as time to
be spent with Him.

I realized that "busy" helped me to feel productive, but
"busy" was also a temptation which was leading me
away from God's best plan.

I had lost precious moments from my parenting that I
would never get back. I had surrendered opportunities
to rest with an enjoyable book or take a nap. I could go
on and on, but most of all I was too "busy" to "BE
STILL" and to "KNOW" that He was God.

His desire is "stillness" for our lives and it something
that we should value daily as well as pursue passion-
ately. We should take pleasure in "being still" in

the presence of an Almighty God. Our ability to hear His voice increases when we are "still." Remember that the Lord is a powerful God who speaks to our hearts in a "still" small voice (Lord Almighty Revelation 1:8).

Prayer

Dear Heavenly Father, help me to prioritize and pursue time with you daily. Help me to be still in your presence and to know that you are my God.

Amen.

The All Sufficient One

a. 2 Corinthians 12: 9

b. 2 Timothy 3: 16 – 17

c. 2 Corinthians 9: 8

d. 2 Corinthians 3: 5

e. Philippians 4: 9

NOTES

ABOUT THE AUTHOR

Pastor Cynthia Allen Shelby is a believer in Jesus Christ who has dedicated her life to learning, growing, and living through scripture. She has served as Youth Leader, Pre-Marital Counselor, and a Life Group Leader with Senior Pastor Donald Adkins at Family Worship Center Church. Her love for praying for others, led her to join the Altar Ministry 30 years ago. She and husband, Pastor Stanett R. Shelby Sr., have served as Altar Ministers and have developed and trained leaders for Christian ministry for most of their ministry. Recently, the Lord transitioned Pastor Cynthia's heart from Altar Ministry to build and establish her latest passion, Perceive Ministries.

She founded the Guilt Free Women's Book/ Bible Studies in 2012. Her vision for teaching women began as a "stirring" to connect with other women according to the Titus 2 mandate. Eight years ago, the book-study styled Life Group formed in her home and transitioned into a Bible study group, which ministered to women throughout the Kentucky, Ohio and Pennsylvania area. In establishing Perceive Ministries, she has hosted a multi-generational Prayer Summit, Leadership Vision

Trainings, Strategic Prayer Calls, Corporate Prayer and Fasting Initiatives, Online Inspirational Devotionals and Behold Women's Conferences.

Pastor Shelby holds a Bachelor of Arts (BA) in Journalism/Advertising and a Master's degree in in Educational Leadership (M. ED.) from the University of Kentucky. She has obtained a Principal's Licensure for Grades K-12 in the state of Kentucky and has been a public/ private-school educator for over 20 years. In addition, she has completed two years of study through Word of Faith Bible School using the curriculum of Rhema Bible Training Center. She resides with her husband, of twenty-seven years, Pastor Stanett R. Shelby Sr. and their two beautiful children Stanett Jr. (20 yrs. old) and Sydney (16 yrs. old) in Lexington, Kentucky.

**Publishing People of Influence
onto Platforms for Impact.**

The Lord gives the word [of power];
the women who bear and publish [the news]
are a great host. Psalm 68:11 AMPC

www.DivineFlowPublishing.com

www.ingramcontent.com/pod-product-compliance
Lightning Source LLC
Chambersburg PA
CBHW021140090426
42740CB00008B/868